ETHNIC DIVERSITY
IN CATHOLIC AMERICA

ETHNIC DIVERSITY
IN CATHOLIC AMERICA

HAROLD J. ABRAMSON

A WILEY-INTERSCIENCE PUBLICATION

JOHN WILEY & SONS, New York • London • Sydney • Toronto

Library of Congress Cataloging in Publication Data:

Abramson, Harold J
    Ethnic diversity in Catholic America.

    "A Wiley-Interscience publication."
    Bibliography: p.
    1. Catholics in the United States. 2. United
States—Foreign population. I. Title.
E184.C3A14   301.45′1   73-1882
ISBN 0-471-00180-5

Printed in the United States of America

10 9 8 7 6 5 4 3 2 1

TO MY MOTHER
AND
THE MEMORY OF MY FATHER

ACKNOWLEDGMENTS

Most of the data in this book are secondary analysis, derived from survey research conducted by the National Opinion Research Center at the University of Chicago in the winter of 1963–1964. The original project, called the Parochial School Study, was financed by a grant from the Carnegie Corporation with supplementary support from the Office of Education of the United States Department of Health, Education, and Welfare.

The substance of Chapter Six has appeared previously in my article, "Ethnic Diversity within Catholicism: A Comparative Analysis of Contemporary and Historical Religion" (*Journal of Social History,* vol. 4, pp. 359–388, Summer 1971); parts of Chapter Seven have appeared in my study, "Inter-ethnic Marriage among Catholic Americans and Changes in Religious Behavior" (*Sociological Analysis,* vol. 32, pp. 31–44, Spring 1971). I wish to acknowledge permission to reprint these articles in their revised form.

The early work in the preparation of these data was carried out while I was a Training Fellow at NORC and a graduate student in the Department of Sociology at the University of Chicago. For their continuing guidance and support, through stages of graduate seminars, the dissertation writing, and the development of this monograph, I am very much indebted to my advisors: Professors Andrew Greeley, Peter Rossi, and David Street. For their encouragement from the beginning and for many memorable discussions on the subject of ethnicity, I am also indebted to my friends and colleagues in sociology, Edward Noll and Joseph Spina.

During the preparation of the manuscript, this study profited from the insightful and detailed comments of Jeffrey Hadden and Richard Hamilton.

Assistance in other forms was also offered by a number of people. I would especially like to thank my good friends Robert and Ethel Coleman for making a writing place available for me; Gale Cottrell for her efficient typing of the manuscript; Rebecca Lehmann for her superior editing; Eric Valentine and Valda Aldzeris of John Wiley and Sons for their generous and friendly help in producing this book; and, above all, my wife Carol for her questions and her answers, her faith and constancy, and a decade of good cheer.

HAROLD J. ABRAMSON

Mansfield Center, Connecticut
January 1973

CREDITS

Acknowledgment is gratefully extended to the following publishers for permission to reprint from their works:

Atlantic-Little, Brown: from *The Middle Americans* by Robert Coles and Jon Erikson, 1971.

Harper and Row: from *Christianity in a Revolutionary Age* by Kenneth Scott Latourette, Volumes I and III, 1958; and from *The Great Hunger* by Cecil Woodham-Smith, 1962.

Harvard University Press: from *Ancestors and Immigrants* by Barbara Miller Solomon, 1956; and from *The Emergence of Liberal Catholicism in America* by Robert D. Cross, 1958.

McGraw-Hill Book Company: from *Children in the Political System* by David Easton and Jack Dennis. Copyright 1969 by McGraw-Hill, Inc. Used with permission of McGraw-Hill Book Company.

Mouton and Company: from *Language Loyalty in the United States* by Joshua A. Fishman et al., 1966.

Routledge and Kegan Paul: from *Christian Democracy in Western Europe 1820–1953* by Michael P. Fogarty, 1957.

University of California Press: from *Custom and Politics in Urban Africa* by Abner Cohen. Originally published by the University of California Press, 1969. Reprinted by permission of The Regents of the University of California.

University of North Carolina Press: from "Unity and Diversity in Modern America" by Robin M. Williams, Jr., in *Social Forces*, Volume 36, October 1957.

University of Notre Dame Press: from "The Americanization of Catholicism" by Joseph H. Fichter in *Roman Catholicism and the American Way of Life*, edited by Thomas T. McAvoy, 1960; and from *The Conservative Reformers* by Philip Gleason, 1968.

The Viking Press, Inc.: from *Little Novels of Sicily* by Giovanni Verga, translated by D. H. Lawrence. Copyright 1925 by Thomas B. Seltzer, Inc., 1953 by Frieda Lawrence. Reprinted by permission of The Viking Press, Inc.

H. J. A.

CONTENTS

Part One

The Sociology of Ethnicity and Religion

CHAPTER ONE

DIVERSITY IN AMERICAN CATHOLICISM

We act as if we wanted Americanization to take place only on our own terms, and not by the consent of the governed.... We are not dealing with static factors, but with fluid and dynamic generations. To contrast the older and the newer immigrants and see the one class as democratically motivated by love of liberty, and the other by mere money-getting, is not to illuminate the future.

RANDOLPH BOURNE (1920)

So we keep coming back to our religious origins—Luther, Calvin, Cromwell, Wesley, and the prophets of Israel—not to mention the Catholicism of the New World, a Catholicism subdivided by racial jealousies far more extreme than ours, and yet less actually Roman than Irish, German, or French-Canadian.

ANDRÉ SIEGFRIED (1927)

FIFTY YEARS AFTER the mass immigrations from Europe, after the tumult and the violence of xenophobia, after federal legislation against foreign movement into the United States, ethnicity has been rediscovered. And in the midst of the reawakening, we find that we know next to nothing about the persistence and changes in the ethnic composition of America. We know that there have been changes, but we do not know how extensive these changes are. We also know that ethnicity frequently assumes new forms, but we do not know what forms ethnic groups in the United States have taken. And most of all, we know that American ethnic groups have not assimilated into a mythological melting pot and emerged as pale or robust copies of the Anglo-Saxon Protestant, but we do not know the basic facts about the nation's pluralism or the extent to which ethnic changes do indeed vary.

The contemporary movements of ethnic assertion among America's blacks, Chicanos, Puerto Ricans, and native Indians remind us once again and inevitably that cultural diversity is the hallmark of the American people, the *sine qua non* ingredients of the society. Karl Deutsch (1966) and others have pointed out that extensive attention has been paid to persisting ethnic components of nationalism and nation-building. But the study of the more subtle, shifting character of the nation's ethnic groups caught up in the development of American society is, as Andrew Greeley (1971) has argued, long overdue.[1]

It is in the interest of comparative ethnic research and of providing some basic facts and patterns of ethnic change and continuity that this book was written. The theme is ethnic diversity—the cultural and social diversity of the Catholic Americans. Far more than any other religious body, Catholicism illustrates the ethnic and sociocultural heterogeneity of the American people. For within this group—about one-fourth of the national population—we can locate the sources that reflect the American experience: the ethnic traditions from many cultural backgrounds, the representatives of old and new and continuing migrations, the array of social class memberships that stratify the society, and the phenomenon of ethnic variation in regional settlement.

Despite countless references to diversity and a cliché-based superficial awareness of the ethnic factor in the American system, the role of ethnicity in Catholicism and its role in the larger society have seldom been the object of

5

probing study. Unity and the consensus of different value systems, rather than diversity and ethnic cleavage, have more frequently been the subjects or expectations of sociological and historical thought. This has been true even in periods when ethnicity seemed more visible for more groups and was defined by national origin and language and region as well as the broader distinctions of race and religion.

A half-century ago, George Santayana (1924, p. 168) described the social context of being an American and reflected that view of the rapidly changing society which was more patient, more tolerant, and more democratic. "If there are immense differences between individual Americans," he wrote, "yet, there is a great uniformity in their environment, customs, temper, and thoughts. They have all been uprooted from their several soils and ancestries and plunged together into one vortex, whirling irresistibly in space. . . . To be an American is of itself almost a moral condition, an education, and a career."[2]

Santayana saw the American as a symbol, and this idea corresponds with (if it is not always equal to) the assimilated results of the myths and ideals of the melting pot, of Anglo-conformity, and of the Americanization movement (Gordon, 1964, pp. 84–159). But in order to understand the nature of symbolic uniformity in America, we require some greater feeling for and knowledge of the extent of diversity. We can choose to alter the perspective and say, if there is considerable uniformity among the masses of Americans, yet there is also a history and a present of immense differences. We can investigate American society in terms of its differences as well as its uniformities, and *then* we may begin to wonder at the way in which it has all been put together and how this kind of pluralism operates.

We can hardly argue that we have attained any real appreciation of the diversity of American society and its fabric of multiple group affiliations. We can hardly offer an understanding of the way in which such diversity has persisted and changed. As bases for comprehending American behavior, sociology has provided us with comparative analyses of the network of social class systems, the role of religion, and the factor of politics, for example, but our perceptions of American society through the influence of ethnicity are limited, at best.

ON SOCIOLOGY AND ETHNIC GROUPS

For any analysis of the ethnic diversity so characteristic of America's past and present, it is difficult to imagine a more opportune phenomenon than the role and status of the Catholics of the United States. Just as striking, however, is the relative lack of sociological inquiry into the social and cultural variations of Catholic Americans, either as ethnic groups or as a specific religious affiliation in the United States. Several major factors have contributed to this condition.

First, ethnicity itself as a conceptual area in social theory has only rarely been examined in any direct and sustained manner; the major contributions have been historical and fairly brief.[3] Our sociological knowledge of ethnicity and ethnic groups derives mainly from scholarship with a tangential focus. The tradition of community studies, as in the work of Caroline Ware (1935), Elin Anderson (1938), W. Lloyd Warner and Leo Srole (1945), and Herbert Gans (1962), provides some insight into the local meaning of the ethnic group in its given time and place in American society.

The studies of assimilation, such as the earlier work of Julius Drachsler (1921) and the more recent analyses of S. N. Eisenstadt (1954) and Milton Gordon (1964), are also important sources for an understanding of ethnicity. And investigations into other conceptual or institutional areas, including analyses by Joshua Fishman (1966) and Stanley Lieberson (1970) on language, Lawrence Fuchs (1956) and Raymond Wolfinger (1965) and Michael Parenti (1967) on politics, or Kenneth Clark (1967) and Gerald Suttles (1968) on the urban community, all have a great deal of relevance to the subject of ethnicity.

Although these different approaches are themselves valuable to the subject of ethnic groups, their usefulness to theoretical questions is variable. In this connection, Milton Gordon's study of assimilation is one of the more important references, not only for his review of the literature on the different predictions of ethnic life in the United States, but also for his discussion of the factors of race, religion, and national origin, providing the components of a basic sense of ethnicity, or "a shared feeling of peoplehood," with a past, present, and future collective orientation (Gordon, 1964, p. 24).

Explicit in Gordon's work is the contribution of religion and national origin to the diversity of American society, but there has been little empirical exploration into the nature of religioethnic behavior. Despite the recurrent and suggestive ideas of H. Richard Niebuhr (1957), Robin Williams (1957), and J. Milton Yinger (1963), among others, the study of religion and ethnicity in America has suffered neglect.

This suggests a second important reason why ethnic diversity within religion is seldom studied. Much of this development stems from the sociological assumption that ethnicity, as defined by national origin, is dead or has at least lost salience in the United States for many areas of social behavior, and especially for religion. This assumption, in turn, rests heavily on the Ruby Jo

Reeves Kennedy (1944, 1952) studies of intermarriage in New Haven. These were the provocative expositions of the "triple melting pot," which was the phenomenon of interethnic marriage occurring increasingly within the boundaries of each of the three major religious affiliations, but with relatively little intermarriage crossing Protestant, Catholic, or Jewish lines.

Kennedy limited the question of the relevance of ethnicity to mate selection, and the studies were based on data from only one city, but the findings were an exciting reformulation of intergroup relations and they provided a basis for subsequent speculations. The best known of these was Will Herberg's (1955) elaboration of the tripartite system of religious identification in the United States. According to Herberg, the forces of the melting pot in American society had virtually eliminated the relationship of religion and nationality. Swedish Lutherans and British Anglicans now identified themselves simply as Protestant Americans, German Jews and Russian Jews would see themselves as Jewish Americans, and the traditional distinctions between Irish and Italian Catholics had faded and merged into the larger body of Catholic America. If any specific character could be said to have emerged within American Catholicism, Herberg argues, it would be along the lines of the dominant Irish model (Herberg, 1955, p. 157).

Following Herberg's assumption of homogeneous religion, Gerhard Lenski (1961) also discounts the ethnic factor and examines the role of white and black Protestantism, Catholicism, and Judaism in modern America, each distinguished mainly by the influence of social class factors. Ironically, the discounting of ethnicity as a source of differentiation within American religion inhibits our understanding, not only of the question of its persistence in any specific areas, but also of the process of social change. We cannot really come to appreciate Herberg's thesis of the Americanization and secularization of religious life by ignoring historical diversity, just as we cannot adequately understand Lenski's test of the influence of the Protestant Ethic on contemporary religionists in Detroit without some control for the extent of preexisting ethnic and cultural diversity within the different religious systems.[4]

In the sociology of ethnicity that has predominated in the United States, the focus has seldom been on religion, and even less on Catholicism. In most of the studies cited here, the relationship of ethnicity to Catholicism is quite incidental; the ethnic groups described may or may not have happened to be Catholic. It has only been relatively recently that anything of a more systematic and comparative nature has been attempted on the subject. Nathan Glazer and Daniel Patrick Moynihan (1963, 1970) helped to shift sociological inquiry in this direction by comparing the distinctiveness and changes characteristic of New York's Catholic Irish, Italians, and Puerto Ricans as well as the city's communities of blacks and Jews.

Their book, *Beyond the Melting Pot*, was important for more than its thesis of the persistence of a form of ethnic life; in some central aspects, such as religion and politics, it compared ethnic groups among themselves rather than to some vague model of Anglo-Americanism. The Irish, Italians, and Puerto Ricans of New York are Catholic ethnic groups, and their roles within their religion and the larger society can be described in this context: not as deviant to the mainstream of American life, but as viable and sustaining forces in themselves.

The idea of ethnicity as deviant to Anglo-American norms leads to the confusion that everybody is "ethnic" in the United States except those with Anglo-Saxon Protestant background. This of course is absurd, if ethnicity is defined as a shared, conscious or subconscious, feeling of peoplehood, based on common referents of racial, religious, national, and/or regional identification. White Americans with an Anglo-Saxon Protestant background have their own national and regional ethnicity.[5] The term "ethnic group" is not to be confused with the meaning of the "minority group," which not only has its own ethnicity but also the disabilities of the minority: less power, lower status, and the stigma of not being culturally presupposed in the larger society. In pluralized societies, the political, social, economic, and cultural presuppositions are usually those that adhere to the ethnicity of the dominant group, in America's experience, those values and life styles of Anglo-Saxon Protestantism.

The idea that ethnicity then usually belongs to some other group, outside of the Anglo-American mainstream, leads to a third factor in explaining the scant attention that American sociology has given to the study of Catholics as ethnic groups, or the analysis of certain ethnic groups as Catholics.[6] This problem is related to the extensive anti-Catholic bias, as Robert Cross describes it, which has persisted in American society long after the end of mass immigration and into the post-World War II years (Cross, 1958, p. 208):

> Discouragingly, this anti-Catholicism is confined to no one class or section, but is to be found in northern industrial states like Massachusetts, where Catholics constitute a majority; in southern areas, where only a handful are to be found; among simple folk, still wary of the Whore of Babylon; and among the best educated, for whom opposition to the Church is a respectable substitute for anti-Semitism; all these "Protestants and Other Americans" have been able to "unite" against Catholicism, as on no other issue.[7]

Ironically, anti-Catholicism has existed within the social sciences as well, and the bias served to depress much interest by non-Catholics in the study of the religion and the Church. The origins of sociology in the United States are imbued with nativist and ethnocentric ideology and practice. Barbara Miller Solomon (1956, pp. 127–128) writes of the racism of the period, in describing the efforts of Francis Walker to combat the movement of "the beaten people of beaten races" from polluting America with social problems and overpopulation:

> Significantly, they accepted not only Walker's economic arguments but also his "racial" condemnation of the existing immigration. From the 1890's to the 1920's social scientists—especially Edward Bemis, Thomas N. Carver, John R. Commons, Davis R. Dewey, Richard Ely, Franklin Giddings, Jeremiah Jenks, William Z. Ripley, Edward A. Ross, and Richmond Mayo Smith—either directly or indirectly gave aid, counsel, or moral support to the work of the Immigration Restriction League.... As emigrants poured in, the professors of economics, sociology, and government directed their attention toward these Europeans. The nation was a unique laboratory for the study of ethnic qualities; never had the superiority of the old stock appeared more evident.[8]

The immigrants were predominantly Catholic and Jewish, and the specific ethnic groups were discussed and catalogued by the Anglo-Saxonist intellectuals in horrific language, calculated to arouse greater efforts for immigration restriction. One of the more biased books, *The Old World in the New*, by Wisconsin sociologist Edward A. Ross (1914), is abundant testimony to the antiforeign mood among the social scientists in the first decades of the twentieth century. Ross, a progressive who believed strongly in radical social and economic reform, was not able to tolerate or understand the presence of cultural diversity in his own country, although he could write intelligently of the social problems of ethnic peoples abroad (Ross, 1915, 1921, 1923).[9]

The antiforeign Anglo-Saxonist movement in the social sciences did not sweep up everybody. Among the minority who did not subscribe to the emotional outpouring of contempt and condescension was Emily Greene Balch, whose *Our Slavic Fellow Citizens* is as dispassionate, empirical, and thoughtful on the subject of the immigrants as Ross' work is the opposite. The Balch book came out in 1910, four years before the publication of the Ross essays, but the Midwestern progressive was apparently uninfluenced by the well-developed arguments of the woman from New England.[10] The dominant ethnocentrism of the period in the sociology of immigration was blind to objectivity.

The pervasiveness of anti-Catholicism in America, with a foundation in the nineteenth century, developed still further from this movement of Anglo-Saxonism at the time of the new immigration (Cross, 1958; Higham, 1963). Among progressives and reform-minded non-Catholics, fear persisted that Catholicism was hostile to the liberal traditions in the United States, and these apprehensions probably contributed to inactivity or indifference to scholarship concerning Catholic ethnic groups. In other words, as the twentieth century progressed, Catholicism in the United States was identified by liberals with the symbolic reaction of Father Charles Coughlin more often than with the social reform of Monsignor John Ryan.[11]

Obviously related to this broad problem is the role of the intellectual life within American Catholicism, and the strains between liberals and conservatives in dealing with it (O'Dea, 1958; Cross, 1958, pp. 146–161). Certainly the debate over secularity within religious education, and the lack of representation of Catholics in the developing social sciences, had much to do with the lag in the empirical study of Catholic ethnic groups by Catholic scholars themselves. Monsignor John Tracy Ellis' term "self-imposed ghetto mentality" helps to explain much of the lack of intellectual life in American Catholicism, for it summarizes the militant stance taken by Catholics against nativism and Know-Nothing forces in the nineteenth century, as well as the persisting and pressing tasks of absorbing the different cultural styles and needs of millions of Catholic migrants throughout the waves of immigration (Ellis, 1955; Hofstadter, 1969, pp. 136–141).

Finally, a fourth factor to help explain the lack of study of ethnicity is ideological. In the egalitarian society of the United States, ethnicity in the form of ascribed racial, religious, national, or regional background is not supposed to matter, and this belief manages to prevail despite the evidence to the contrary. Ethnicity has mattered. Ideological emphasis on achievement and the dynamics of a fluid class system is and has been normative in American social science, whereas ethnicity is more frequently rejected as "local color," exotic, and ephemeral at best, or tradition-bound, parochial, and reactionary at worst. In either event, ethnicity is defined as deviant to the reality and expectations of the American life style.

The assimilationist bias in American sociology and history, which happens to fit in well with the course of anti-Catholicism but is distinct and separate from it, has dominated the scholarship. Blatant exceptions to the myth apparently have always been understood, implicitly or explicitly, for America's blacks, the descendants of a slave-caste, as well as for native Indians and the colonized Mexican-Americans in the Southwest.

For white groups of newer or older immigrations, and for Asian cultures in the United States, however, ethnicity is *expected* to disappear, not only because of acculturation and the wider currents of assimilation, but also because social class and status based on achievement require this to happen. That the two forces of class and ethnicity work together in America, and not always in the same way for all ethnic backgrounds, is not a prevalent idea. Social scientists themselves have ignored ethnicity, in part because of this ideology of presumed uniformity, but also because of their own feelings of ambivalence or for their more subjective dispositions that ethnicity is not important to *them* (Greeley, 1971; Vecoli, 1970). The important idea of American pluralism as a result of the interaction between social class and ethnic attachment will be discussed more fully in the concluding chapter of this book.

PROCEDURE AND SOURCE OF DATA

The sociological aspect of ethnic diversity among Catholic Americans is limited in this book to social and religious dimensions. The relationship of ethnicity to the demographic background of Catholic Americans is described. Where do the different ethnic groups live? How Eastern are the Irish, and how Midwestern are the Germans? What is the exact nature of differential migration periods? To what extent are the different ethnic backgrounds first, second, and later generation in the American experience? Are there any groups that show signs of continuing migration into the United States? Just how urban are the different ethnic backgrounds in America, and which groups reflect a rural or small-town setting? What are the educational and occupational patterns of change and continuity for the Irish, the Poles, and the French-Canadians? How much social mobility has there been for the Germans and the Italians?

The ethnic factor is also analyzed in the context of marital assimilation. Exactly how much intermarriage is taking place among Catholic Americans? Are there different rates of exogamy for the different generations, and when intermarriage does occur, are there any patterns of choice for those of Eastern or Western European backgrounds? Which factors are most likely to influence the selection of a spouse?

The association between ethnic culture and religion is examined by contemporary and historical analysis of different nationality groups. What are the different characteristic levels of involvement within Catholicism? Does generation in this country really make a difference for the cultures of Catholicism, and if so, is the pattern the same for all groups? What explanation is there for the varieties of religious practice and association that are Irish, or Italian, or Polish? What happens to these traditions, which the immigrant groups brought with them, in the light of an American experience of cultural and marital assimilation within the Church? What effect does intermarriage with other Catholic groups have on traditional ethnic behavior?

Finally, there is a discussion of the changes and continuities in terms of American society and an experience of diverse class memberships and ethnic attachments. What are the sociological implications of the ethnic mosaic for an understanding of the American experience? These are some of the questions this book deals with, primarily through empirical evidence.

Much of the data cited here were obtained from a national survey of white Catholic Americans interviewed by the National Opinion Research Center in 1964.[12] The universe sampled is the total noninstitutionalized white Catholic population of the United States, 23 to 57 years of age. The sample is limited to those respondents who identified themselves as Roman Catholic in reply to a question on current religious preference. The total sample size numbers 2071 respondents drawn from a standard multistage area probability sample.

Questions asking for national background supply the data on ethnicity. Respondents were asked for the main nationality background of their fathers and mothers, and if they were married, of their spouses' fathers and mothers.[13] Ten specified nationality backgrounds are presented in the original data: English (includes Scottish, Welsh, English-Canadian, and English-Australian); Irish; Italian; German (includes Austrian and Swiss); French-Canadian (includes a very few French and Belgian); Scandinavian (includes Danish, Norwegian, and Swedish); Polish; Lithuanian; all other Eastern European nationalities combined; and Spanish-speaking (includes Puerto Rican, Mexican, and a few of Spanish and Portuguese origins).

Table 1 offers the distribution of born-Catholic respondents by the ethnicity of their Catholic fathers and mothers.[14] Since the rank order of distribution is the same in both columns and the size of the percentage is approximately the same for each ethnic group in the two columns, there is no apparent evidence of size bias dependent upon the sex of the parent. The five largest ethnic groups, each of which is more that 10 per cent of the Catholic population, are the Italians, the Irish, the Germans, the Poles, and the French-Canadians. Fairly detailed analysis of these five groups is facilitated by their predominance in the population.[15]

The combined Eastern European and Spanish-speaking categories, each of which is 7 or 8 per cent of the Catholic population, are next in order of size. The Eastern Europeans, excluding the numerous Polish Catholics who were considered as an individual category, are too disparate a group for meaningful detailed analysis on the level of nationality, but preliminary comparison and description will include this combined category. The Spanish-speaking, the majority of whom are Puerto Ricans and Mexicans, share similar cultural backgrounds and pose less of a substantive problem than Eastern Europeans by being combined in the data. Nevertheless, for future studies of the ethnic factor in America, it would be imperative to seek large enough samples to avoid combined categories and thereby have independent data for the Hungarians, the Czechs, the Slovaks, and other groups not often found in comparative analysis.

The last three groups listed in Table 1—the English, the Lithuanians, and the Scandinavians—are the smallest in the born-Catholic population of

Table 1. Ethnic Distribution of Born Catholics, by National Background of Catholic Fathers and Mothers (In Percentages)

Nationality Background	Respondent's Father	Respondent's Mother
Italian	20.9	19.7
Irish	17.3	16.5
German	15.9	15.6
Polish	11.0	11.9
French-Canadian	10.4	10.3
Eastern European	7.6	7.7
Spanish-speaking	7.3	7.4
English	3.2	3.7
Lithuanian	2.7	2.6
Scandinavian	0.5	0.8
Other Backgrounds	3.2	3.8
Total	100.0	100.0
	(1,602)	(1,726)
N =	1,602	1,726
Converts, NA conversion =	252	252
Non-Catholic parent =	186	58
Don't know =	27	30
No answer =	4	5
Total =	2,071	2,071

the United States. The English and the Scandinavians, mainly Protestant in religion, would be expected to have very few Catholics among their fellow nationals; data in this study are not available on the conversion status of parents and grandparents, but it is most likely that many English and Scandinavian Catholics in the United States are descended from converts to the Church. The Lithuanian Catholics, although numerous enough to be distinctive vis-à-vis other Eastern European groups, are still quite small a group in relation to the national distribution. The English and the Lithuanians provide too few respondents for any extensive analysis and will be compared only in the descriptive stages with the larger Catholic groups. The negligible Scandinavian Catholics will be excluded altogether.

The sample is limited to nominal Catholics at the time of the survey. Thus the data do not account for any born-Catholics who have since fallen away from the Church. Former Catholics are therefore not represented in the subsequent study of social and religious diversity. This fact of leakage is an important problem, but there is little reason to suspect a relationship, and therefore a source of bias, between apostasy and ethnicity. Gerald Shaughnessy's (1925) work on the subject of immigration and Catholic growth in the United States focuses on evidence that gives an affirmative answer to the question of his book's title, *Has the Immigrant Kept the Faith*? He suggests no peculiarly ethnic association with leakage in past decades. More recently, moreover, in a study of college students and the relationship of religion and career choice, Andrew Greeley (1963) points out that Catholics have the lowest overall rate of apostasy among American religious groups, and he finds no positive correlation between ethnicity and departure from the Church.

A larger methodological problem exists which bears on the framework and data of this study. There is the question of survey research and secondary analysis: the use of data to study some specific aspects of social behavior which were not the primary concerns of the original survey design. In this case, the basic project was interested in the contrasts between Catholic Americans who attended parochial schools and those who received a public education (Greeley and Rossi, 1966). Fortunately, by virtue of a comprehensive interview schedule, the major questions of direct concern to this analysis of ethnic diversity are available: data on ethnic background, marriage choice, measures of associational religious involvement, and important control factors of social and religious influence.

On the other hand, some information that would further clarify the meaning of ethnic diversity is missing. Questions on foreign languages spoken in the home, the size of the ethnic group in the respondent's neighborhood, the number of ethnic friends and associates, the nature of voluntary associations, and other relevant aspects of ethnic attachment would have contributed to a still greater understanding of the role of ethnicity within Catholicism. The comparative meaning of ethnic identity and the ethnic community waits for future research on the ethnic factor in American life.

The nature of secondary analysis from survey research therefore is restrictive, and the study is necessarily limited to certain specific aspects of social and religious diversity among Catholic ethnic groups. To supplement and clarify the findings of the survey data, especially for the sources of ethnic diversity, historical analyses are offered. Although there is an all-too-frequent ahistorical approach in American sociology, I hope that a combined use of survey research with historical analysis may contribute something toward understanding the roots and development of contemporary behavior and social change.

The major assumption of this book rests with the ethnic factor, as it has provided a social basis of diversity for American Catholicism, not altogether unlike the denominational factor in American Protestantism (Niebuhr, 1957; Glock and Stark, 1965; Hadden, 1969) or the nationality factor in historical and contemporary Judaism (Glazer, 1957; Rischin, 1962). Part Two of this book refers to social diversity: the distribution of ethnic differences throughout the backgrounds of Catholic Americans, the extent of ethnic marriage, and the demographic and religious background factors that generate marital assimilation or, conversely, contribute to the maintenance of ethnic endogamy and group life.

Part Three examines religious diversity: the traditional religioethnic orientations of different Catholic groups, the historical patterns that have advanced the religious traditions brought by immigrants to the United States, and the changes in religious behavior which emerge as the ethnic groups assimilate within American Catholicism. Part Four considers the larger question of ethnic pluralism and the wider meaning and implications of cultural diversity in the United States.

NOTES

1. Within the last few years, increasing numbers of books on the ethnic factor in the United States have been making their appearance, in response to the charges of neglect. Some are historical (e.g., Gleason, 1968; Greene, 1968; Luebke, 1969; Allswang, 1971). Others are polemical, such as the recent work of Schrag (1970), Novak (1971), and Levy and Kramer (1972). Still others are discursive and sociological on the subject of many groups together (Feinstein, 1971; Greeley, 1971), or on the treatment of single groups individually as with the Prentice-Hall Ethnic Groups in American Life Series (e.g., Kitano, 1969, on the Japanese, and Fitzpatrick, 1971, on the Puerto Ricans) and the Random House Ethnic Groups in Comparative Perspective Series (which includes Killian, 1970, on the White Southerners, and Lopreato, 1970, on the Italians).

2. The philosopher Santayana's thoughts were consistent with other writers who took a more positive view of the results of mass immigration. The negative disposition was more prevalent, however, for it resulted in restrictive legislation in 1924. See the discussions in Solomon (1956) and Higham (1963).

3. In the two-volume set (1500 pages) of *Theories of Society*, under Part Two of Volume One, "Differentiation and Variation in Social Structures," there are only two selections dealing with ethnicity. This contrasts sharply with the other "ascriptive solidarities" presented: five selections each for kinship, primary groups, and territorial community. (See Parsons et al., 1961, pp. 267–404).

The problem of the research on ethnicity in social theory is cited by Parsons (1961, p. 268) in an editorial foreword: "We have treated ethnic solidarity as an extension of the reference point of kinship. Though it is a very important theme in social analyses, there have been few attempts to treat it in really general terms. . . . Because the available space here is so limited, only a token recognition of the importance of the problem was possible."

For major contributions on the meaning of ethnicity, see Weber, "Ethnic Groups" (in Weber, 1968, pp. 385–398); Wirth, 1945; and Francis, 1947. Recent works that emphasize the theoretical aspects of ethnic groups in society, rather than the meaning of ethnicity, are Shibutani and Kwan (1965), van den Berghe (1967, 1970), Blalock (1967), and Schermerhorn (1970).

Social scientists have also become increasingly concerned with the theoretical implications of ethnicity and cultural pluralism in area studies of Africa and the Caribbean. See, for example, Dotson and Dotson (1968), Kuper and Smith (1969), Argyle (1969), and Cohen (1969).

4. Bernard Rosen (1962) was the first to point this out in his review of Gerhard Lenski's *The Religious Factor*.

5. Relatively little work has been done on the meaning of Anglo-Saxon Protestant ethnicity. See Baltzell (1966), Anderson (1970), and Killian (1970). Other viewpoints are presented by Schrag (1970) and Novak (1971).

6. Specific attention to the ethnic factor within Catholicism is found in only a few serious studies. See Nuesse and Harte (1951), Fichter (1960), Rossi and Rossi (1961), Greeley and Rossi (1966), and Abramson and Noll (1966). More general treatments on American Catholicism which acknowledge that ethnicity is no longer relevant follow the Herberg (1955) perspective. See, for example, La Farge (1956) and Liu and Pallone (1970). For a bibliography of the literature in the sociology of religion, which reveals little emphasis on the relationship between ethnicity and religion, including Catholicism, see Berkowitz and Johnson (1967). In American history too, the study of ethnicity in American life has been ignored. Relatively little deals with religioethnic conflict, or the role of the ethnic factor in American Catholicism. For some general statements on this problem, see Vecoli (1970).

7. See also Billington (1964) on the origins of American nativism. Much of the anti-Catholicism has eased considerably since 1960 and the election of John F. Kennedy to the Presidency. For the literature of the twen-

tieth century which is critical of the Roman Catholic Church in the United States, see two classic portrayals of different stripes: William Lloyd Clark's *The Story of My Battle with the Scarlet Beast* (1932) and Paul Blanshard's *American Freedom and Catholic Power* (1949).

8. See also the discussion in Baltzell (1966).

9. In Ross' autobiography, *Seventy Years of It*, he discusses some of his earlier work and says, "In an article . . . I characterized some of our immigrants from Eastern Europe as 'the beaten members of beaten breeds.' I rue this sneer" (1936, p. 277). Despite the apology, his book still manages to reflect the patronizing condescension of the earlier period. For more extensive discussions of Edward Ross and the intellectual antiforeign movement he symbolizes, see Goldman (1952), Solomon (1956), Higham (1963), Gossett (1965), and Baltzell (1966).

10. For a description of this minority point of view, which the Balch work (1910) represents, see Solomon (1956, pp. 176–194). Ironically, Ross knew of the Balch study, for he cited one reference to her work, alluding to the Polish community in Hadley, Massachusetts. Unfortunately, Ross' reference was misleading and out of context. See Balch (1910, p. 328) and Ross (1914, p. 127).

11. For a vivid and critical contrast between these two priests, see Shannon (1963, pp. 295–326) and the discussion in Cross (1958) and Greeley (1969, pp. 219–250). The somewhat estranged relationship between the liberal tradition and American Catholicism, historically, is not unlike that described by Morris Janowitz (1959, pp. 11–24) on the relationship between social science research and the military.

12. The sampling procedure and the questionnaire are described in detail in the final report of the survey. The study's primary aim was the examination of the social and religious effects of Catholic parochial schooling. See Greeley and Rossi (1966).

13. Multiple responses were allowed on the nationality questions, and these cases (40 respondents) will be excluded from the analysis here, along with the nonsubstantive categories (Other, No Answer, and Don't Know).

14. Table 1 presents the order of ethnic groups by the ranking of percentages. This is the basis for ordering ethnic groups in all of the tables of this book. Thus the order will change from one table to the next, because the percentage sizes change with each discussion.

15. The sampling procedure used in this survey (Greeley and Rossi, 1966) undersampled Catholics in those regions of the United States where Catholics are fewer in the total population, such as in the South and the

West, and oversampled in regions more heavily Catholic, such as in New England. As a result, the figures for the Spanish-speaking, particularly the Mexican-Americans, underrepresent the actual size of this group in the national population (Grebler, Moore, and Guzman, 1970); similarly, the figures for the French-Canadians are probably overrepresentative. On the bases of the percentages shown in Table 1 and the estimated total Catholic population given for 1970 (from the *Official Catholic Directory*), approximately 48 million, the rough estimations of the sizes of the different Catholic ethnic groups can be offered to the nearest hundred thousand:

Italians	10,000,000	Spanish-speaking	3,500,000
Irish	8,300,000	English	1,500,000
Germans	7,600,000	Lithuanians	1,300,000
Poles	5,300,000	Scandinavians	200,000
French-Canadians	5,000,000	Others	1,500,000
Eastern Europeans	3,600,000	Total	47,800,000

Part Two

Social Diversity
among Catholics

CHAPTER TWO

THE ETHNIC FACTOR
IN CATHOLIC AMERICA

...as a concrete social category, "Catholic" includes a wide spectrum of class and ethnic affiliations.... The unity of ritual, the adherence to religious authority, and the creedal commitments are vitally important for an understanding of Catholicism in America. But the Church in its temporal, institutional, social aspects is far from the monolithic structure sometimes depicted, and its central anchors of unity do not preclude a certain pluralism of specific social orientations to real and immediate problems of men in communities, states, and the nation at large.

ROBIN M. WILLIAMS, JR. (1957)

ONE OF THE GREATER PROBLEMS in the study of ethnicity is the fact that it so often is confused and confounded with larger social aspects of the society. Is ethnic behavior actually a reflection of other factors? How can we distinguish ethnicity from other background variables, such as generation in the United States, region of the country, or, indeed, the influence of social class and status. To bring some order into this maze of competing explanations and expectations, it is necessary to provide a clearer picture of the socioethnic background of Catholic Americans. The purpose of this chapter is a more precise description of the social characteristics of Catholic ethnic groups in the United States.

The first chapter emphasized the question of ethnic diversity within American Catholicism, and one of the problems frequently encountered is the assumption of homogeneity within broad religious affiliations (Herberg, 1955; Lenski, 1961). The lack of relevant data with enough cases for a wide sample of any religious community is, of course, a key problem in the study of religious and ethnic diversity. The national census data would be extensive enough, but the census omits any questions on religions and the specific ethnic background of respondents' grandparents. The availability here of a national sample of Catholic Americans helps measurably to overcome this problem, by facilitating the description and analysis of ethnicity and religion across a range of different regions, settlements, and class backgrounds. How diverse are Catholic Americans when we consider ethnic *and* social characteristics in our society?

IMMIGRATION AND GENERATION IN THE UNITED STATES

As background to socioreligious behavior, the establishment of ethnic diversity is not in itself sufficient; ethnicity is very often related to distinct periods of immigration history. Table 2 presents what is probably the most salient factor, and certainly the most often discussed, for the Catholic population of the United States: generation of residence in this country. The fact of the relationship is demonstrated quite clearly.[1]

Table 2.   Per Cent Distribution of Catholic Ethnic Groups, by Generation in the United States

	Generation in the United States			
Ethnicity	Third or Later	Second	First	Total
English	69	29	2	100 (49)
Irish	69	25	6	100 (269)
German	65	30	5	100 (243)
French-Canadian	46	42	12	100 (154)
Polish	34	63	3	100 (170)
Eastern European	23	67	10	100 (120)
Italian	16	76	8	100 (331)
Spanish-speaking	12	42	46	100 (115)
Lithuanian	10	76	14	100 (42)
Total	41	49	10	100 (1,493)

$$N = 1,493$$
$$\text{NAP ethnicity} = 38$$
$$\text{DK} = 41$$
$$\text{NA} = 3$$
$$\text{Total} = 1,575^a$$

^{a} The total N of 1,575 represents the working case total for all tables in this chapter. It is the sum of all born-Catholics with Catholic parents, as follows:

$$N = 1,575$$
$$\text{Converts, NA converts} = 252$$
$$\text{Non-Catholic fathers} = 186$$
$$\text{Non-Catholic mothers} = 58$$
$$\text{Total } N = 2,071$$

Defining length of residence in this country into the first generation (the respondent is foreign-born), second generation (the respondent has one or both parents who are foreign-born), and third generation or earlier (the respondent has both parents born in the United States and up to all four grandparents native-born as well), the data of Table 2 show the proportions of each ethnic group falling into each generational category.

The total figures for the entire Catholic population reveal only 10 per cent to be foreign-born, reflecting the quota system enacted in 1924 and the end of mass immigration. A more important fact, however, is the percentage of Catholic Americans who are of the second generation. Half of the entire population have one or both parents born in the country of origin. Combining the first and second generations, a majority of nearly 60 per cent are this close to the immigration experience. On the basis of this fact alone, one can question the assumption of a unified, homogeneous religious group. But even more important, the recency of immigration varies with ethnicity, as the body of Table 2 indicates.

The ethnic groups divide clearly between the second and third generations and reflect the distinctiveness of the earlier and more recent waves of immigration (Hansen, 1940; Handlin, 1959). The English, the Irish, and the German Catholics predominate in the earlier periods of immigration to the United States; about two-thirds of each of these three groups is at least third generation. A still more refined analysis of the relationship of ethnicity to generation would indicate even more clearly the well-known precedence of the English Catholics in American society (Abramson, 1969, p. 230). A more detailed breakdown of the generation factor shows that nearly half (47 per cent) of the born-Catholics of English origins had three or four grandparents who were native to the United States, in marked contrast to corresponding percentages of 31 for the Irish, 27 for the Germans, 25 for the French-Canadians, 7 for the Spanish-speaking, 6 for the Poles, 5 for the Eastern Europeans, 3 for the Italians, and 2 for the Lithuanians. Data in the study on the conversion status of parents and grandparents are not available, but it is most probable that many of the English Catholics in the United States are descended from converts to the Church. This would help explain the general similarities of the English Catholics to the larger, older, Anglo-Saxon elements of the American population.

In the last great immigration wave, which began around 1890 and continued until the beginning of the restrictive 1920s, the Italian, Polish, Lithuanian, and other Eastern European groups are found. The figures of Table 2 complement those for the nationalities of the earlier period; two-thirds or more of the Southern and Eastern Europeans are second generation, the children of the immigrants. Inevitably, much that follows in this book will be strongly related to this fact.

Whereas only 10 per cent of all Catholics are foreign-born, the Spanish-speaking stand out as the exception. Nearly half of this group is not native-born to the mainland United States. This reflects of course the recent and continuing migration of Puerto Ricans into the mainland population and the movement of Mexicans across the border. The absence of travel restrictions for Puerto Rican citizens and the proximity of Mexico facilitate such migrations.

It may also be noted here that the 12 per cent of the French-Canadians who are first generation is not any different from the total percentage. The decline in emigration of French-speaking Canadians is noteworthy, considering the closeness of Quebec to the United States, and especially to New England. The explanation, however, lies in the rise of industrial opportunities for the semiskilled and working classes of Quebec (the movement of the past 20 years from rural Quebec has been to Montreal and not to the United States), as well as the decline in such opportunities in New England and other regions of the United States (Hughes, 1963). The same pattern cannot be said to exist for the Spanish-speaking groups, the Puerto Ricans and the Mexicans (Glazer and Moynihan, 1963; Christian and Christian, 1966; Grebler, Moore, and Guzman, 1970; Fitzpatrick, 1971).

This general summary of the association between ethnicity and generation, although sometimes ignored, is not unexpected. Hutchinson (1956), among others, has provided detailed analysis of the composition of the immigration periods and the distribution of nationalities among the different generations of Americans. The intention here is the documentation of the extent of diversity within the total Catholic population. Ethnicity within the Church is affected still further by the length of residence in the country, and this fact will be of great importance to the subsequent analysis in the chapters to come.

REGIONAL DISTRIBUTION

So much of the writing on Catholic Americans refers to their regional concentration in the Northern and Eastern states that further reporting and description here might seem unnecessary. Aside from scattered references and impressions of the distinctive nationality enclaves resident in particular areas, however, there has been no comparative examination of specific Catholic ethnic groups in a national context. Table 3 summarizes these impressions by relating ethnicity to region and answers the question of where the particular ethnic groups have settled and now reside. The focus is on the nationality rather than the region, and the percentages are run in the direction of the groups themselves. There are six regions presented, each comprising standard member states according to United States Census designations.[2]

The data of Table 3 clearly substantiate the common assumption about the American Catholic population: nearly three-fourths of the total group live in New England, the Middle Atlantic states, and the East North Central region, all in the Northern and Eastern sectors of the nation. Only a minority resides in the South and the West.

Ethnic diversity by region is not always as widely understood. Some groups have strong regional associations. The French-Canadians, for example, predominate in New England; a majority of 52 per cent resides in this one region alone. This is not unexpected, in view of the proximity of Quebec and the industrial development of New England textile factories and mills in

Table 3.   Per Cent Distribution of Catholic Ethnic Groups, by Region of the United States

| | Region of the United States | | | | | | |
Ethnicity	New England	Middle Atlantic	East North Central	West North Central	South	West	Total
French-Canadian	52	6	22	9	3	8	100 (166)
Lithuanian	39	21	34	2	2	2	100 (42)
English	22	26	22	6	12	12	100 (51)
Irish	22	39	18	5	8	8	100 (276)
Italian	10	62	16	1	3	8	100 (335)
Polish	5	30	42	10	7	6	100 (175)
Eastern European	3	49	24	12	5	7	100 (122)
Spanish-speaking	3	20	8	0	7	62	100 (117)
German	1	23	30	25	8	13	100 (253)
Total	15	34	23	9	6	13	100 (1,537)

$$N = 1,537$$
$$\text{NAP ethnicity} = 38$$

$$\text{Total} = 1,575$$

the last century, which provided labor demand and emigration opportunities (Ducharme, 1943; Theriault, 1960). This group is considerably underrepresented in the Catholic areas of the Middle Atlantic states and follows national Catholic norms more or less proportionately in the remaining regions.

The smaller Lithuanian group, on the other hand, does not have a majority of its membership in any one particular region. The Lithuanians are more than twice as likely to be resident in New England (39 per cent) as is the general Catholic population (15 per cent), and they are also well overrepresented in the East North Central states. In all other regions the Lithuanians are underrepresented, and in the South and West, they are virtually strangers to the resident populations.

The English Catholics show still another settlement pattern. They are the earliest among Catholic immigrants, as well as the group descended from many converts to the Church, and they are fairly well distributed throughout all regions in approximation to the national norms. The English are twice as numerous in the South as other Catholics (12 per cent residing there), and they are somewhat less represented in the Middle Atlantic states of New York, New Jersey, and Pennsylvania, which is the region with the largest proportion of the Catholic population—34 per cent. English Catholics, then, experience invisibility, not only because of their cultural similarities with

Anglo-Saxon Protestants but also because of their settlement behavior. They do not stand out markedly in any particular region of the country.

In contrast to the English, the Irish do stand out by region. They are, characteristically and visibly, Easterners. As many as 61 per cent of the Irish Catholics are inhabitants of the six states of New England and the three states of the Middle Atlantic. With their predominance in these two regions, their proportions in the rest of the country tend to fall below the pattern of the total Catholic population.

The Italians also have a strong regional association. They are over-whelmingly concentrated in the states of the Middle Atlantic region; 62 per cent of the Italian Catholics live in New York, New Jersey, and Pennsylvania. No other group, with the exception of the Spanish-speaking in the West, has as high a proportion in a singular regional enclave. Because of this concentration, the Italians are not as proportionate as other ethnic groups in the rest of the country. Only 1 per cent of the Italian Catholics, for example, live in the West North Central states, and only 3 per cent reside in the South.

Both the Polish and other Eastern European Catholics, unlike the Lith-uanians, are underrepresented in New England, but they are predominant in the Middle Atlantic and East North Central regions. Well over half—over 70 per cent— of these two groups live in these two areas. A plurality of the Poles (42 per cent) resides in the East North Central region, while nearly a majority of the Eastern European category (49 per cent) comes from the Middle Atlantic states. Their presence elsewhere in the country is approximately consistent with the general Catholic population.

The Spanish-speaking, as already mentioned, show a majority of 62 per cent of their numbers residing in the West. Although the data do not permit a specific distinction between the Puerto Ricans and the Mexicans, this regional breakdown suggests that the 69 per cent of the Spanish-speaking in the South and West are most likely of Mexican or Hispano descent, whereas the majority of the 31 per cent living in the Eastern and Northern states are probably of Puerto Rican background. Grebler, Moore, and Guzman (1970) point out that most of the Mexican Americans live in five states, designated in their work as the Southwest: Arizona, California, Colorado, New Mexico, and Texas. And as the 20 per cent Spanish-speaking figure for the Middle Atlantic region indicates, the greater number of the Puerto Ricans inhabit New York, New Jersey, and Pennsylvania, with the vast majority in New York City (Fitzpatrick, 1971).

The German Catholics do not show a pattern similar to any of those already discussed. They are overwhelmingly Midwesterners. In fact, 55 per cent of the Germans are located in the two North Central regions, as op-

Table 4.   Per Cent Distribution of Regional Settlement in the United States, by Catholic Ethnic Group

Ethnicity	U.S. Total	New England	Middle Atlantic	East North Central	West North Central	South	West
Italian	22	15	38	15	4	10	14
Irish	18	27	19	14	11	25	12
German	16	1	11	22	47	22	17
French-Canadian	11	37	2	10	11	6	7
Polish	11	4	10	21	13	13	6
Eastern European	8	2	11	8	11	7	4
Spanish-speaking	8	2	4	3	0	9	36
English	3	5	3	3	2	7	3
Lithuanian	3	7	2	4	1	1	1
Total	100	100	100	100	100	100	100
	(1,537)	(226)	(536)	(354)	(133)	(89)	(199)

$$N = 1,537$$
$$\text{NAP ethnicity} = 38$$
$$\text{Total} = 1,575$$

posed to the 32 per cent of all Catholics who live there; and only 24 per cent of the German Catholics reside in the more eastern Middle Atlantic and New England states, in contrast to a figure of more than twice that size for the total Catholic population. A surprising point, it might be noted, is the mere 1 per cent of all German Catholics to be found in New England. The contrasting association of German Catholics with the Midwest is historically documented and suggests differentials in other background characteristics, which will be examined in this chapter.[3]

Because of the different sizes of these ethnic groups, it can be misleading to discuss their settlement patterns just by looking at the regional distribution within each group. It would also be important to know, for example, whether a given nationality, which may concentrate its own members in a particular region, is also numerous in relation to *other* ethnic groups in that region. Size then becomes the focus, and Table 4 helps answer this question by changing the direction in which the percentages are run. The distribution is now presented in terms of regions instead of nationality backgrounds.

In New England, for example, the most numerous groups are indeed the French-Canadians and the Irish, as the prior discussion indicated. But the

Lithuanians, who are overrepresented among themselves in New England, do not stand out in Table 4 as a large New England ethnic group because of their small size in the total Catholic population.

In the Middle Atlantic states, the Italians represent four out of every ten Catholics. Table 4 confirms the impression that not only do the Italians predominate as a group in New York, New Jersey, and Pennsylvania, but they also predominate among all Catholics in these states. Because of their size, the Irish are the next largest group in the Middle Atlantic region. And because of their relatively fewer numbers, the Eastern Europeans do not emerge as a large group within this region, despite the fact that half of those Catholics with this background do reside there.

The East North Central states reflect a regional ethnic microcosm of the Catholic American population. Every nationality background is represented, no particular ethnic group stands out in relation to other groups, and the rank order of size is roughly that of the national distribution.[4] If any ethnic background is more numerous in this region, it is the Polish group; the Poles are nearly twice as frequent in this region as they are in the total population.

Moving on to the West North Central region, consider the surprising proportion of German Catholics. As noted earlier, the Germans as a group tended to settle in the Midwest. But because of the relatively fewer Catholics there in general, the Germans account for nearly one out of every two Catholics of whatever nationality background. It may also be noted that the German ethnic proportions, in Table 4, form a curvilinear pattern from east to west, peaking in the West North Central region. This would indicate not only a settlement route, moving westward from New England and the East, but also an increasing ethnic visibility in the context of other Catholic nationality groups.

Table 4 then shows the French-Canadian and Irish predominance in New England, the Italians and the Irish in the Middle Atlantic states, the position of the Germans in the West North Central region, and the representation of the Spanish-speaking and Chicanos in the West. Although the Spanish-speaking group comprises only 8 per cent of the total Catholic population in this sample (this includes the Puerto Ricans), they are 36 per cent in the Western states, 19 percentage points higher than the next largest Catholic group, the Germans.

The South not only has the lowest proportion of Catholics in its population, but it also lacks, as a region, any particular Catholic ethnic stamp. Its ethnic composition is predominantly Anglo-Saxon Protestant and black. The East North Central states, on the other hand, have the second highest proportion of Catholics, but they share with the South the fact that no particular ethnic visibility is pronounced. The differences between these two regions are the size of the Catholic population, the North-South disparities, and the fact that more has been written about Catholics in the East North Central region.

Joseph Fichter (1960) has briefly compared these two regions in an essay on the Americanization of Catholics. He proposed that the size of any minority will influence the effect which the more dominant culture has on the members of that minority:

> Unfortunately we have no "pure type" of large Catholic minority in the United States to demonstrate this proposition. The Mexican Catholics of the Southwest and the Irish Catholics of the Northeast have carried ethnic overtones so that in these cases we must talk about the Americanization of the Mexicans and Irish, rather than Americanization of Catholics. The small minority of Catholics in some of the Southeastern States serves as a better example of this principle. Here we find the scattered Catholics almost totally assimilated to the dominant regional culture on all scores except religion. . . . The thesis is perhaps best demonstrated among Midwestern Catholics. In this area there has never been a predominantly hyphenated Catholicism. None of the Catholic immigrant groups, Poles, Italians, Germans, Irish, has been large enough or solidaristic enough, to put a peculiar foreign stamp on Catholicism. All of them together have not formed a large and isolated minority that prevented mingling with the dominant non-Catholic majority. . . . The result is that Midwestern Catholicism has achieved a degree of American maturity not yet approached by Catholics in other parts of the country.

Fichter (1960, p. 121) argues here for the importance of size as a crucial variable. But his assessment of the role of predominant single or multiple ethnicities seems just as important. It might be informative to compare, historically, the sociology of Catholic-Protestant relations in each of the four regional structures suggested by the foregoing discussion: (1) predominant concentrations of a single ethnic group in regions of relatively few Catholics (the Germans in the West North Central states, the Mexicans in the Southwest); (2) predominant concentrations of a single ethnic group in regions of relatively many Catholics (the Italians in the Middle Atlantic states, the Irish and the French-Canadians in New England); (3) multiple ethnicities in a region of relatively few Catholics (the South); and (4) multiple ethnicities in a region of relatively many Catholics (the East North Central region).

First, one may expect that the social and cultural behavior of a religious group and its individual members will evolve differentially under conditions where the size of the group, as Fichter has pointed out, is variable. Furthermore, one may consider the attitudes and dispositions of the larger society toward the specific religious group under conditions where the larger community views the religion as being singularly ethnic or, on the other hand, as pluralistically mixed. Is Catholicism known locally as the "German church," "the Mexican church," or "the Irish church"? It is reasonable to expect that, given the specifically ethnic stamp and its cultural peculiarities, more can be learned about the cultural varieties of religion as well as the variability with which the larger society views American Catholicism.[5]

I am drawing away from the immediate interests of this section. The intention of this chapter is the documentation of the extent of diversity. What has been evident in this section is the phenomenon of particular regional association with Catholic ethnic groups, not unlike the regionalism that has long characterized the American experience. As a macrosociological concern, regionalism seems to have ended unfortunately with the works of Howard Odum (Odum and Moore, 1938) and other scholars (Jensen, 1951). A renaissance of interest in regionalism, as well as ethnicity, may prove particularly fruitful for sociology, perhaps not always to describe the persistence of national diversity but to assess the nature of change from the American past.

URBAN AND RURAL SETTLEMENT

As a source of diversity, regionalism often relates to the size of settlement. Table 5 presents data on the kind of hometown in which Catholic Americans

Table 5. Per Cent Distribution of Catholic Ethnic Groups, by Size of Hometown

Ethnicity	Size of Hometown				
	Large City or Suburb	Small City	Small Town	Farm and Open Country	Total
Polish	53	21	13	13	100 (169)
Irish	46	29	16	9	100 (274)
Italian	43	20	31	6	100 (335)
English	30	28	36	6	100 (50)
German	26	17	25	32	100 (253)
Lithuanian	19	48	21	12	100 (42)
Eastern European	18	29	40	13	100 (121)
Spanish-speaking	12	27	41	20	100 (117)
French-Canadian	10	48	25	17	100 (167)
Total	33	27	26	14	100 (1,528)

$$N = 1,528$$
$$\text{NAP ethnicity} = 33$$
$$\text{NA hometown} = 14$$

$$\text{Total} = 1,575$$

are raised, and it confirms the common impression that the Catholic population of the United States is an urban population. One-third of the total group
was raised in the largest cities—metropolitan areas with a population of 1/2
million or more. The next category shown, smaller cities (designating those
whose population ranges from 10,000 up to 500,000), claims 27 per cent of
all Catholics. Together the urban population among Catholics accounts for
six out of every ten.

Although this majority is decidedly urban in background and contributes
to the reputation of Catholic Americans, it nevertheless tends to deemphasize
the other side of the coin. Table 5 also shows that 40 per cent of this population were raised in small towns (no larger than 10,000 in size), in the open
country, and on farms. Although not a majority, this percentage is meaningful.

Furthermore, the table points out that ethnic groups within Catholicism
do not all show similar hometown backgrounds. The most urban of the
groups are the Polish Catholics, 53 per cent of whom were brought up in the
largest metropolitan areas. The two other most urban ethnic groups, with
pluralities of their members from the largest cities, are the Irish and the Italians.

Two of the backgrounds come mainly from the smaller cities, as opposed
to the largest urban areas. Nearly half of the French-Canadians and the Lithuanians were raised in cities of intermediate size, anywhere from 10,000 to
500,000 in population. The category of the "smaller city" is admittedly difficult to conceptualize in this set range, but it is useful in its differentiation
from the more urbanized metropolitan areas.

The small town, as defined, is more manageable. In towns of 10,000 or
fewer people, Table 5 shows 40 per cent of the Eastern Europeans, 41 per
cent of the Spanish-speaking, and 36 per cent of the English. All of these percentages exceed the proportion of the total Catholic population raised in small
towns, and they are pluralities of frequency for the groups themselves.

If the small town is combined with the still more rural category of
farm and open country, the Eastern Europeans and the Spanish-speaking
groups both display a majority of their members raised in rural environments. For the Eastern Europeans (and it is difficult to speak meaningfully
about this mixture of nationality backgrounds) there is a rural total of 53
per cent. The comparable figure for the Spanish-speaking is even higher, 61
per cent. Since this group is nearly half first generation (as Table 2 pointed
out), this suggests that for the Spanish-speaking immigrants, the points of
origin are the rural settlements and villages of Mexico and Puerto Rico
(Mills, Senior, and Goldsen, 1950; Padilla, 1958; Rubel, 1966; Grebler,
Moore, and Guzman, 1970; Fitzpatrick, 1971).

The third group with a rural background are those of German ethnicity. A majority of 57 per cent of the German Catholics claim nonurban roots. Indeed, a third of all Germans were brought up on farms and in the open country. This is over twice as many of the entire Catholic population reported to have been raised under the same rural conditions.

It should be fairly clear at this point that Catholic Americans, when examined by ethnic background, show a remarkable diversity in the type of rural or urban environment in which they were raised. This diversity may be summarized by emphasizing the highlighted traits of the preceding findings of this chapter. Combining the size of hometown with specific national region and the generation of residence in the United States, the different ethnic groups show the following characteristics.

The Irish are mainly third or earlier in generation, the grandchildren or great-grandchildren of immigrants, and are resident of the largest cities of the East, such as Boston, New York, and Philadelphia.[6] The German Catholics are also of the earlier generations but were brought up on farms and in the rural towns of the Midwest, in such counties as Eau Claire (Wisconsin), Barber (Kansas), Madison (Nebraska), and Towner (North Dakota). The French-Canadians are fairly evenly divided between the second and third generations, the children and grandchildren of the immigrants from Quebec, and were raised in the smaller cities and towns of New England, such as Manchester, New Hampshire, and Waterbury, Connecticut.

The Italians from Southern Europe, and the Poles, Lithuanians, and other Eastern Europeans, are predominantly second generation, the native-born children of immigrant parents. Their settlement patterns differ, however, after this similarity. The Poles were reared in the largest cities of the East North Central region, in the urban areas of Chicago, Detroit, Cleveland, and Milwaukee. The Italians are resident of the largest cities of the Middle Atlantic states, predominating in the metropolitan areas of New York, Newark, and Philadelphia. The Lithuanians were brought up in the smaller cities of the East North Central and New England regions, in places like Gary, Indiana, and Waterbury, Connecticut. And the Eastern Europeans, as a composite group, were raised in the small towns of less than 10,000 population in the Middle Atlantic states, such as those illustrated by the coal-mining towns of Carbon and Northumberland counties in eastern Pennsylvania.

The two remaining ethnic groups are perhaps the most visible and least visible within the Catholic population. The former, the Spanish-speaking, are more apparent in contemporary America for several reasons. Whether Chicano or Puerto Rican in origin, they have a relatively greater physical dissimilarity to the Anglo-American appearance than other Catholic Americans have, and they have experienced and endured extensive prejudice and discrimination as ethnic groups, both historically and in the present. They are visible, too, in their recent efforts at group organization in fighting discrimination in the 1960s and 1970s. But they are also visible because, as this chapter shows, almost half of the Spanish-speaking are the first generation on the mainland United States. In contrast to all other Catholic backgrounds, the Puerto Ricans and the Mexicans are the closest to the immigration experience. Accordingly, they retain the Spanish language and much else of Puerto Rican and Mexican culture. And, finally, they are apparent in a national context of visibility, because of their regional concentration: the Mexicans and Hispanos in the cities and towns of the Southwest, and the Puerto Ricans in the urban centers of the East.

The least visible ethnicity within American Catholicism belongs to the English, for fairly obvious reasons. As noted previously, the generational experience of the English Catholics is third or earlier. Aside from the fact that many of the English Catholics are in all probability descended from Anglo-Saxon Protestants who converted to the Church, the English are also fairly evenly distributed throughout all regions and stand out in no particular association with the size of the town in which they were raised. Thus their invisibility is due not just to cultural similarities with the Anglo-Saxon Protestants but also to their regional assimilation and their distributed settlement patterns.

Analysis of the background of the English Catholics proves useful in contrast to all of the other groups. The exception to distinctiveness appears to make the existence of diversity all the more remarkable. In a sense, this is not unlike deviant case analysis; the English are ethnically a part of the larger heterogeneity of American Catholicism, but they are deviant to the idea and reality of being visible in American society and thereby are a standard by which the heterogeneity and visibility of other ethnic groups may be appreciated. Except for their religion, the English Catholics have direct kinship to the Anglo-Saxon Protestants. The Irish and the Germans may share a similar generational past with the English, but the Irish in the United States are visible, in part, because of their traditional urban and Eastern experiences, and the Germans are visible because of their rural and Midwestern associations. To be sure, the discussion thus far has been limited to three demographic variables, but some of the persistence of the ethnic factor is due to the configurations of these historical patterns which still prevail. The remaining portion of this chapter now will deal with two important measures of socioeconomic status, the relationship of ethnicity to occupation and education.

OCCUPATIONAL PATTERNS

Historical references to the occupational structure of Catholic Americans have dwelled on the positions of blue-collar labor: craftsmen, different kinds of operatives and factory workers, and the manual labor of the semiskilled and the unskilled. These were the inevitable occupational opportunities for immigrant workers in a developing industrializing society (Handlin, 1951, pp. 63–93).

John Higham (1963, pp. 16, 114) points out how dependent American industry was on immigrant labor at different time periods:

By 1870 about one out of every three employees in manufacturing and mechanical industries was an immigrant—a proportion which remained constant until the 1920's. . . . Employers acquired a larger appreciation of the value of southern and eastern European immigrants, and by 1909 the latter comprised a third or more of the entire labor force of the principal industries of the country.

More recent studies have undertaken to chart the occupational mobility of Catholic Americans from blue-collar to white-collar jobs (Greeley, 1963; Warkov and Greeley, 1966). As the economic structure of the society altered its demands and opportunities for increased education became available, more and more Catholics of the second and third generations assumed higher positions of socioeconomic status, in the presumably classic American style.

The extent to which ethnicity is an influential factor in differentiating American Catholic occupational behavior, and thus contributes to the notion of diversity, remains to be clearly appreciated. Both past and present occupational patterns are important for comparative ethnic considerations, and both will be examined here for the two generations of Catholic respondents and their parents.

To arrive at some idea of the nature of the employment of Catholic Americans, Table 6 compares the occupational background of the Catholic population with that of the national labor force. Two roughly comparable populations are examined: the national labor force of 1910 with the occupational background of the respondents' fathers, and the national white male labor force of 1960 with the occupations of the male respondents (and spouses of female respondents) themselves.

A number of facts are clear from the data of Table 6. First, there is strong confirmation of the point that the Catholic immigrants provided the industrial labor required by the developing society. Of the Catholic fathers, 62 per cent had various blue-collar occupations, as opposed to 48 per cent of the total national labor force in these jobs. Indeed, Catholics were twice as likely to be craftsmen, and one and a half times as likely to be operatives.[7]

Table 6.   Per Cent Occupational Distribution of National and Catholic Labor Forces: 1910, 1960, and Catholic Generations

Major Occupational Category	National Labor Force 1910[a]	Catholic Parental Generation (Fathers)	National Labor Force 1960[b]	Catholic Respondent Generation (Males)
White collar	22	24	38	43
Professional	5	3	11	12
Managerial	7	15	12	12
Clerical	5	3	7	13
Sales	5	3	8	6
Blue collar	48	62	54	53
Craftsmen	12	23	21	17
Operatives	14	21	21	20
Service	10	5	6	8
Other Labor	12	13	6	8
Farming	30	14	8	4
Farm manager	17	12	6	2
Farm labor	13	2	2	2
Total	100	100	100	100
		(1,527)		(988)

N = 1,527 N =   988
NAP ethnicity =   35   NAP female =   534
NA occupation =   13   NAP ethnicity =   24
                            NA occupation =   29

Total = 1,575   Total = 1,575

[a] Data for 1910 from Palmer and Miller (1954, pp. 83–92). Based on all gainful workers.
[b] Data for 1960 from U.S. Bureau of the Census (1961). Based on experienced civilian labor force (white male).

Interestingly enough, the percentage white collar in both the Catholic parental and the 1910 total labor forces is the same. The breakdown by white-collar categories points to the explanation; Catholics of this period were less likely to be in the professional, clerical, and sales positions (since they lacked the educational prerequisites), but they were twice as likely (15 per cent) to be in managerial occupations as were those of the total labor force (7 per cent). Since the managerial classification includes the proprietors of all kinds of business establishments, the small retail shops, grocery stores, and restaurants of many of the immigrant groups help to contribute to the percentage white collar.

The differential provided by the proportions of blue-collar workers in both populations is matched by the difference in those of farming backgrounds. Nearly one-third of the national labor force was engaged in agriculture in 1910, and this is more than twice the proportion of Catholics with farming occupations (14 per cent). The difference is especially marked in the farm labor category. Catholic immigrants came to work in the industrialization of the society; agriculture was the estate of the native-born.

A second point of Table 6 is the extent of change for both populations in the two time periods. In fact, the increase in white-collar positions is somewhat higher between the two Catholic generations than it is between the national labor forces of 1910 and 1960. For Catholic Americans, the proportions in both blue-collar and farming occupations show their decline (whereas for the national labor force, it is only farming that experiences a big decline between 1910 and 1960). The occupational mobility so often alluded to is clearly substantiated here.

How much ethnic differentiation is there in the occupational background of Catholic Americans? Table 7 offers some answers to this question. Consider first the jobs that the fathers of the respondents had. For white-collar positions, the English and the Irish of this parental generation both show the highest proportions, of over one-third. The remaining percentages range from the 26 per cent of the Italians (reflecting this group's proprietorship of stores and restaurants) to the low of 12 per cent of the Polish Catholics in white-collar jobs.

Most of this generation, as already noted, worked in different kinds of blue-collar categories. It is especially true for the more recent immigrants from the countries of Southern and Eastern Europe. The German Catholics and the Spanish-speaking have relatively fewer blue-collar antecedents, in contrast to all other nationality backgrounds (the majorities of whom have blue-collar jobs), because of their concentration in agriculture. Thirty-nine per cent of the fathers of Puerto Ricans and Chicanos were engaged in farming, mostly in their native villages and the rural areas of Puerto Rico and Mexico. The Germans report 31 per cent of their fathers in farming, and because they are mainly third generation or even earlier in the United States, the agricultural background was Midwestern rather than European.

There is no other diversity evident in the data for the fathers in Table 7, given the fairly gross categories of "white collar" and "blue collar." A clear majority of every ethnic group, except the agricultural German and Spanish-speaking Catholics, had fathers in blue-collar work.

Moving to the contemporary generation and the data for the male respondents in Table 7, there is a wider range of differentiation in the percentage white collar among ethnic groups. The Irish and the English are the

Table 7. Per Cent Distribution of Catholic Ethnic Groups, by Occupation of Fathers and Male Respondents, and Percentage Change in Occupational Background from Parental to Respondent's Generation

Ethnicity	Occupation of Fathers				Occupation of Male Respondents				Percentage Change in Occupation		
	White Collar	Blue Collar	Farming	Total	White Collar	Blue Collar	Farming	Total	White Collar	Blue Collar	Farming
English	39	57	4	100 (51)	66	31	3	100 (36)	+27	−26	−1
Irish	38	55	7	100 (273)	66	31	3	100 (158)	+28	−24	−4
Italian	26	71	3	100 (333)	48	52	0	100 (223)	+22	−19	−3
French-Canadian	23	67	10	100 (165)	32	67	1	100 (113)	+9	0	−9
German	22	47	31	100 (252)	46	42	12	100 (153)	+24	−5	−19
Lithuanian	19	74	7	100 (42)	45	55	0	100 (31)	+26	−19	−7
Eastern European	16	73	11	100 (119)	24	74	2	100 (87)	+8	+1	−9
Spanish-speaking	16	45	39	100 (117)	18	73	9	100 (72)	+2	+28	−30
Polish	12	77	11	100 (175)	34	65	1	100 (115)	+22	−12	−10
Total	24	62	14	100 (1,527)	43	53	4	100 (988)	+19	−9	−10

$N = 1,527$
NAP ethnicity = 35
NA occupation = 13

Total = 1,575

$N =$ 988
NAP female = 534
NAP ethnicity = 24
NA occupation = 29

Total = 1,575

highest with 66 per cent, and the Spanish-speaking are the lowest with 18 per cent; this shows a considerable range of 48 percentage points. The lower proportions in farming reflect the national decline; the persistence of a minority of the German Catholics in agriculture is noted with their proportion of 12 per cent.

The actual percentages of some of these ethnic groups in white-collar occupations are not necessarily surprising. But the diversity is important. The change, seen in the context of numerous nationalities, is variable. For the parents of this generation of Catholic respondents, the ethnic norm was blue-collar work, but for contemporary Catholics in the United States, there is a suggested phenomenon of different mobility patterns. Table 7 also summarizes these patterns by showing the percentage change in occupational background, from the parental to contemporary generation. Certain comparisons can now be made more easily.

All of the ethnic groups show some gain in the percentage of white-collar jobs between generations, although the gain is indeed variable. The Irish display the greatest increase; from 38 per cent in the parental generation to 66 per cent today, the Irish rose 28 points. Marked increase in this category is also there for the English, the Lithuanians, the Germans, the Italians, and the Poles, the latter two groups with a 22 percentage point gain.

Little gain in the attainment of white-collar occupations is seen for the Spanish-speaking (an increase of 2 points), the Eastern Europeans (8 points), and the French-Canadians (a gain of 9 points). For the Spanish-speaking, however, the pattern is not static; there has been considerable movement out of agriculture (a decline of 30 points) and into the blue-collar jobs (an increase of 28 points). The French-Canadians and the Eastern Europeans, on the other hand, show the least amount of overall occupational mobility in any direction. This lack of movement from the parental to the respondent's generation is difficult to explain in view of the prevalent norm of change and mobility for most Catholics and in light of the wider structural changes of the whole society in the past 50 years.

Part of the explanation may be due to the fact that the French-Canadians and the Eastern Europeans predominate in the smaller cities and towns where economic opportunities are either restrictive or diminishing. The French-Canadians are concentrated in towns and industries that are or have been economically marginal for the recent past, the textile and clothing mills of smaller New England cities. The Eastern Europeans, as noted earlier in this chapter, happen to live in those smaller towns formerly dominated by the coal companies, the settlements of Carbon and Northumberland counties in eastern Pennsylvania. In both situations, the textile mills and the coal towns have their particular historical and contemporary ethnic group concentrations (Ducharme, 1943; Greene, 1968), and their economic stagnancy is reflected by the static occupational patterns of the ethnic groups involved. The level of education attained, discussed next, will bring further clarification to the occupational changes just described.

THE ACHIEVEMENT OF EDUCATION

The demands for widespread public education as a universal right in American society, and the increasing opportunities for such education, coincided with the mass immigration to the United States of the poor and the unlettered. The two phenomena are, of course, not unrelated, but they suggest the general patterns to be found over time in the empirical data. Table 8 depicts the expected relationships between ethnicity and education for the fathers and male respondents of this survey.

The data of Table 8 refer to the highest levels of education attained, as reported by the respondents about themselves and their fathers. The interview schedule does distinguish between public and parochial schooling, and this distinction will be of great importance in subsequent analysis. It is sufficient at this point to compare levels of education, rather than type of schooling, in order to examine general ethnic characteristics.

Referring to the education of fathers, the most important ethnic factor of Table 8 is that which is linked to generation in the United States. The older immigrant groups, the English, the Irish, the Germans, and the French-Canadians, were those that tended to reach higher levels of education at the earlier periods in the century. Only these four groups had proportions that were higher than the 16 per cent of all Catholics who finished high school or went on to college. The majority of the newer immigrants—all Eastern European backgrounds, the Italians, and the Spanish-speaking—reported their fathers as having had a sixth-grade education or less. These findings are consistent with the data on the fathers' occupational backgrounds.

What kinds of change have occurred in the meantime to the children of those who were close to the experience of immigration? Table 8 also looks at the educational levels reported by the male respondents for themselves. Again, there is some evidence of diversity among the ethnic backgrounds in attaining higher education. Looking at the middle columns of Table 8, which offer the percentages of educational level for the respondents, there are 26 per cent of all Catholics in the category of entering college. The spread of differences is considerable, however; the Irish are the highest, with as many as half of their

Table 8.   Per Cent Distribution of Catholic Ethnic Groups, by Educational Level of Fathers and Male Respondents, and Percentage Change in Education from Parental to Respondent's Generation

	Education of Fathers						Education of Male Respondents					Percentage Change in Education			
Ethnicity	6th Grade or Less	7th or 8th Grades	Some High School	All High School	Some College or More	Total	8th Grade or Less	Some High School	All High School	Some College or More	Total	8th Grade or Less	Some High School	All High School	Some College or More
Spanish speaking	71	13	9	5	2	100 (99)	50	22	18	10	100 (51)	−34	+13	+13	+8
Lithuanian	66	14	14	0	6	100 (29)	22	21	21	36	100 (19)	−58	+7	+21	+30
Italian	65	18	10	3	4	100 (247)	20	32	31	17	100 (169)	−63	+22	+28	+13
Eastern European	56	24	9	7	4	100 (90)	27	24	33	16	100 (63)	−53	+15	+26	+12
Polish	55	30	8	5	2	100 (132)	25	24	27	24	100 (75)	−60	+16	+22	+22
French-Canadian	42	28	8	10	12	100 (120)	28	29	26	17	100 (73)	−42	+21	+16	+5
German	33	41	6	13	7	100 (222)	26	13	25	36	100 (115)	−48	+7	+12	+29
English	24	36	11	20	9	100 (46)	4	29	33	34	100 (24)	−56	+18	+13	+25
Irish	13	39	17	16	15	100 (252)	3	13	35	49	100 (112)	−49	−4	+19	+34
Total	44	30	10	9	7	100 (1,237)	22	23	29	26	100 (701)	−52	+13	+20	+19

N = 1,237
DK education = 313
NA education = 5
NAP ethnicity = 20
Total = 1,575

N = 701
NAP females = 862
NAP ethnicity = 11
NA education = 1
Total = 1,575

numbers having some college experience, and the Spanish-speaking are lowest, with only one out of every ten in this same level. The range between these two extreme groups is evident.

Among other groups high in the proportion going to college, in addition to the Irish, are the Germans and the English. Furthermore, the Lithuanians report as many as 36 per cent of their group having some higher education, an unusually high proportion for a predominantly second-generation ethnic group. In fact, the Lithuanians are 12 to 20 percentage points higher on college entrance than any of the other European ethnic backgrounds of the more recent immigration periods.

Given these absolute percentages in levels of education, how do the patterns of educational mobility compare between the two family generations? Table 8 also offers the percentage change in the schooling achieved between the Catholic fathers and their sons. Considering the college level and high school completion, all groups do show some gain. As with their move into white-collar jobs, the Irish display the greatest increase, this time by 34 percentage points, in college entrance. In this last column, the Lithuanians show a difference of more than 30 points, and the Germans a gain of 29. Their length of residence in the United States may help explain the Irish and German movement into higher education, but the later arrivals among the Lithuanians show unusual achievements in education after only a relatively brief duration in America. The fact that nine out of every ten Lithuanian Catholics is either a first- or second-generation American underscores this finding even more.[8]

The least movement into higher education, on the other hand, is shown by the French-Canadians (a gain of 5 points) and the Spanish-speaking (8 points). The occupational changes into white-collar positions for these two groups were also relatively low. The Puerto Ricans and the Mexicans, by virtue of being traditionally in agricultural labor, are moving into blue-collar jobs, whereas the French-Canadians show little occupational movement of any kind. The Spanish-speaking Chicanos and Puerto Ricans are assuming the position of an industrialized proletariat (specifically, those who have left the world of migrant rural labor), without yet moving rapidly into the realm of higher education.

The static quality of the French-Canadians, however, is in terms of both occupational and educational mobility. The Italians, the Poles, and the Eastern Europeans (with whom the French-Canadians share a pattern of little occupational change) all reflect increases in high school completion and college entrance at or near the proportions of the total Catholic population. The French-Canadians, it is noted, do not. The emphasis on traditional qualities and a corresponding disinterest in some of the uses of higher education and social change have been observed for the French-Canadian, although they have not yet been well explained in comparison with other traditional backgrounds (Miner, 1939; Wade, 1946; Rosen, 1959; Hughes, 1963). A good deal more research into the values and persistence of ethnic life, into the meaning that different groups place on tradition, and the degree of success each ethnic group has in retaining its cultural orientations is necessary for fuller explanations.

SUMMARY

A few questions have been raised throughout this chapter which, unfortunately, cannot be adequately answered within the limits of this book; the explanation of ethnic heterogeneity in the many areas of social behavior is the basis of future work on the subject. Nevertheless, the purposes of this chapter have been twofold: to point out the kinds of basic social diversity that do exist, and, having demonstrated these, to consider the differentiating factors for the subsequent ethnic analysis in this book.

There are many similarities and differences among Catholic ethnic groups by the demographic factors of generation, region, and size of settlement. The conventional folk wisdom has it that Catholic Americans are all urban, immigrants or the children of immigrants, and residents of the northeast quadrant of the nation. This of course is the myth that has just been debunked, for it ignores the four out of every ten Catholics from rural areas and small towns, the 41 per cent whose families have been in the United States for three generations or more, and the Catholics who live in many different regions, particularly in regional ethnic enclaves.

There are also many similarities and differences among the Catholic ethnic groups by class factors of occupation and education. Here too generalizations cannot be made for all Catholic Americans, again because ethnicity intrudes. What is true in the total pattern for all Catholics is not necessarily the Lithuanian, French-Canadian, or Irish pattern. Mobility rates as reflections of changes in the world of work and the world of schooling are not uniform and standard for all Catholic groups. Blue-collar jobs in manufacturing, construction, and mining were characteristic of most but not all of the Catholic generations prior to the contemporary population. The Germans, the Mexicans, and the Puerto Ricans each had an agricultural past. And when American society altered its economic structure in the middle third of the twentieth century, the changes for these groups varied too, with the Germans moving into white-collar jobs and the Spanish-speaking taking on an urban blue-collar complexion. Other ethnic groups also changed, moving from blue collar to white collar at their own paces.

In the world of education too, ethnic variation is pronounced. Some groups, like the Irish, the Lithuanians, and the Germans, moved at a faster rate past high school and into college. Other groups, like the Spanish-speaking and the French-Canadians, perhaps because of stronger attachments to their cultures and the use of their traditional languages, showed less educational mobility into the larger schooling system of the society. In all of these cases, the religion masks the underlying ethnic factor.

If ethnicity is to be reckoned with, then certainly the state of ethnic marriage and marital assimilation are crucial questions. The extent of this phenomenon for the national range of Catholic Americans and the diverse ethnic backgrounds involved becomes a critical issue. It is considered in the following chapter on social diversity.

NOTES

1. As noted in Chapter One, note 14, the order of ethnic groups presented in the tables of this book follows the ranking of percentages, in order to highlight a pattern of high-to-low proportions among the different groups shown.

2. Census designations: *New England* states include Connecticut, Maine, Massachusetts, New Hampshire, Rhode Island, and Vermont; *Middle Atlantic* states include New Jersey, New York, and Pennsylvania; *East North Central* states include Illinois, Indiana, Michigan, Ohio, and Wisconsin; *West North Central* states include Iowa, Kansas, Minnesota, Missouri, Nebraska, North Dakota, and South Dakota; *South* includes Alabama, Arkansas, Delaware, District of Columbia, Florida, Georgia, Kentucky, Louisiana, Maryland, Mississippi, North Carolina, Oklahoma, South Carolina, Tennessee, Texas, Virginia, and West Virginia; *West* includes Alaska, Arizona, California, Colorado, Hawaii, Idaho, Montana, Nevada, New Mexico, Oregon, Utah, Washington, and Wyoming.

3. In his history of German Catholics in the United States, Gleason (1968, p. 15) writes: "An examination of the directory [of German-speaking priests in the United States] confirms the popular impression that the German Catholics were most thickly concentrated in the Middle West: Fourteen of the twenty dioceses having fifty or more German-speaking priests fell within the region bounded on the east by Ohio, on the west and south by Missouri, and on the north by Minnesota." See also Barry (1953) and Hawgood (1940).

4. Calculations of Spearman's rank order correlation coefficients, relating each regional column in Table 4 to the United States total, for proportions

of ethnic populations, are as follows: coefficient of .82 for Middle Atlantic; .77 for East North Central; .70 for the South; .62 for West North Central; .60 for the West; and .28 for New England. Thus the Middle Atlantic and East North Central regions are the most similar to the total national distribution, but the sizes of the ethnic groups in the Middle Atlantic states are much more at variance with the national totals.

5. Cultural and religious variations within the Church are taken up in some detail in Chapters Five and Six, but because of the lack of sufficient cases in the survey, it is not possible to pursue the implications of regionalism, ethnicity, and the sociology of minority group behavior in this study.

6. The city and county illustrations, used as examples of locations where the different ethnic groups tend to predominate, are actual primary sampling units for National Opinion Research Center interviewing and were a real part of this national survey of Catholic Americans. See Greeley and Rossi (1966).

7. The comparison here is between specifically designated Catholics and the national labor force (which includes Catholics as well, as all non-Catholic groups). Thus the differences will be somewhat muted, because Catholics are also included in the national labor categories. It suggests also that these differences would be larger if Catholics were not part of the data in the more inclusive labor forces of 1910 and 1960.

8. Sociological study of the relatively small Lithuanian community in the United States, as well as for other smaller groups (such as the Armenians, the Greeks, the Ukrainians, and the Finns), is very much neglected. Research on these groups, their cultural values, their structure, their social mobility and status in postimmigration decades, is quite essential.

CHAPTER THREE

THE STATE OF
ETHNIC MARRIAGE

Before the year 1950 arrives, the children and grandchildren of the immigrants who have entered since 1885 will be distinguished from other Americans only by their surnames, and sometimes by their features and complexion. They will no longer be Poles or Italians or Slovaks, but Americans. They will have intermarried with the original Anglo-Americans, and with other immigrants, so that the generation born in 1950 will contain racial elements quite diverse from any that were present a century before.

JAMES BRYCE (1917)

I'm Polish. I mean, I'm American. My family has been here for four generations; that's a lot. My great-grandfather came over here, from near Cracow. I've never been to Poland. I'll never go there. Why should I? It's in your blood. It's in your background. But I live *here*. My wife is the same, Polish. We're just like other people in this country, but we have memories, Polish memories, that's what my grandfather used to say: "John, don't let your kids forget that once upon a time the family was in Poland." How *could* I forget? My wife won't let me. She says you have to stay with your own people. We don't have only Polish people living near us, but there are a lot. Mostly we see my family and my wife's family on the weekends, so there's no time to spend doing anything else.

ANONYMOUS (Coles and Erikson, 1971)

SOCIOLOGICAL STUDIES OF INTERMARRIAGE in the United States have, since 1950, increasingly emphasized the religious factor. Attention has been paid to the extent, causes, and consequences of marriage outside the religious group (Thomas, 1951; Heiss, 1960, 1961; Haerle, 1962). At the same time, there has been a corresponding decline in attention paid to American ethnic groups and the marriage patterns of Americans of differing nationality backgrounds, for the reasons discussed in Chapter One.

Since the formulation of the triple melting pot idea (Kennedy, 1944, 1952), and the subsequent elaboration on tripartite religious identification in America by Herberg (1955), there has been little sustained effort to explore either the patterns of ethnic marriage or the correlates and changing nature of ethnic religion. Religious intermarriage has subsumed the question of ethnic intermarriage, and the study of comparative religion in the United States has correspondingly neglected the traditional ethnic components.

Given the diversity of American Catholicism, what is the condition of the Catholic melting pot? Some attention has been directed over time to the study of intermarriage rates among different ethnic groups in America, but most of this work is limited to relatively few nationalities and specific regional or urban locations (Drachsler, 1921; Wessel, 1931; Kennedy, 1944, 1952; Thomas, 1956). It is the purpose of this chapter to broaden the inquiry by investigating the extent of ethnic marriage among Catholic Americans as a national population. Rates of endogamy (defined as marriage within the ethnic group) and exogamy (defined as marriage outside the ethnic group) will be presented with the focus on comparative patterns for the different traditional ethnicities sharing the Catholic religion.[1]

The following analysis is divided into two sections: the first looks at the degree of ethnic endogamy or in-group marriage among the different nationality backgrounds; the second points out the extent and nature of ethnic exogamy or out-group marriage taking place between these different Catholic groups. What ethnic backgrounds are more likely to be endogamous, and which tend toward exogamy? What kind of change occurs between the parental and respondent's generations, and how does this change relate to each of the ethnic groups considered? With exogamy across nationality lines, but within a common religious affiliation, what patterns emerge among out-

51

group marriages? These are the basic questions on the issue of marital assimilation among Catholic ethnic groups in the United States, and the answers to these will provide a clearer picture of the Catholic melting pot and the notion of social diversity.

PERSISTING ETHNICITY: THE EXTENT OF ENDOGAMY

It would not be unusual to expect, as the vast literature on America as a melting pot predicts, that the parental generation of contemporary Catholics is more ethnically endogamous than the respondents themselves and, similarly, that the specific groups of the more recent immigration periods are more endogamous than those groups associated with the third or earlier American generations. These two expectations are considered in this section of the chapter.

The extent of diversity among the parents and respondents of the different ethnic backgrounds is shown in Table 9. The first column indicates that the range of ethnic endogamy extends from a high of 96 per cent for the Spanish-speaking parents to a low of 27 per cent for the English. The total proportion of 80 per cent endogamous marriages for all Catholic parents is itself high, but the column refers to the parental generation of contemporary Catholics, the majority of whom (as seen in Chapter Two) are either foreign-born themselves or the children of immigrants. Under these conditions (especially if the marriage took place in the country of origin), ethnic endogamy would certainly be expected.

The Latin and Eastern European nationality backgrounds are clearly the most endogamous, all falling above the 80 per cent level for all Catholics. The remaining four groups, all of Western European origin, are less endogamous, but excepting the English, their proportions still account for a majority; the French-Canadians are 79 per cent endogamous, the Germans 73 per cent, and the Irish 65 per cent. The only group to be predominantly of mixed ethnic marriage in this parental generation are the English; only 27 per cent had spouses of English background, or, conversely, more than seven out of every ten English Catholic fathers had a Catholic wife of some non-English ethnic background.

The data support the expectation of the influence of the period of immigration. The more recently arrived ethnic groups—the Spanish-speaking and those from Southern and Eastern Europe—all indeed show higher proportions of ethnic endogamy. The remaining groups, whose peaks of immigration preceded the waves of the early twentieth century, are marked by somewhat lower percentages.

Table 9.   Per Cent Endogamous of Catholic Ethnic Groups, for Parental and Respondent's Marriages, and Percentage Change in Endogamy from Parental to Respondent's Generation

Ethnicity of Father	Mother of Same Ethnicity	Spouse's Father of Same Ethnicity	Percentage Change in Endogamy
Spanish-speaking	96	88	−8
	(119)	(88)	
Italian	93	66	−27
	(336)	(256)	
Lithuanian	93	50	−43
	(42)	(38)	
Polish	89	50	−39
	(170)	(135)	
Eastern European	86	39	−47
	(124)	(90)	
French-Canadian	79	68	−11
	(153)	(112)	
German	73	45	−28
	(234)	(165)	
Irish	65	43	−22
	(269)	(179)	
English	27	12	−15
	(45)	(27)	
Total	80	55	−25
	(1,492)	(1,090)	

$$N = 1,492 \qquad\qquad N = 1,090$$

NAP ethnicity = 83   Not married = 190

Total = 1,575[a]   NAP ethnicity = 120

Non-Catholic spouses = 175

Total = 1,575[a]

[a] See Footnote *a* in Table 2.

As noted, all groups with the exception of the English show a majority of endogamous marriages. This fact changes when the marriage of the children, or the respondents themselves, are examined. The second column of Table 9 offers the distribution for the contemporary Catholic population. The total proportion for ethnic endogamy is now 55 per cent, but while still a majority, there are only three nationality backgrounds with a distinctly higher percentage: the Spanish-speaking, the French-Canadians, and the Italians, with endogamous proportions of 88, 68, and 66 per cent, respectively.

Further diversity is demonstrated by the range of differences in Table 9 (second column). Two of the Eastern European nationality groups, the Poles and the Lithuanians, are next highest, each with exactly half of their numbers marrying into the same traditional background as their own. The remaining four groups—the English (again last, with only 12 per cent choosing spouses of the same English background), the Irish, the Germans, and the combined Eastern European category—all reveal a minority of endogamous mating.

The Eastern European "group" is difficult to conceptualize here, because it combines many different nationality backgrounds: Czechs, Hungarians, Slovaks, and other Catholic nationalities from Eastern Europe, excluding the Poles and Lithuanians. In Table 9 (second column), the figures for the Eastern Europeans are read to mean that 39 per cent of these Catholics marry other Catholics of one or another Eastern European background (again, excluding the Poles and Lithuanians), and that (the implicit reciprocal) 61 per cent of these individuals marry Catholics of some "non-Eastern-European" background. This latter figure does include possible marriages to Polish and Lithuanian Catholics.

There are some patterns suggested in the change between parental and respondents' behavior, as noted in Table 9. By subtracting the proportion of endogamous marriages between the two family generations shown in the first two columns, Table 9 offers a direct comparison in its third column. Clearly, all nine groups experience a decline in endogamy. Although the fact of decline is consistent, there is nevertheless considerable variability in the extent of loss per ethnic group.

The resulting rank orders of these two family generations of Catholic Americans in the proportions of ethnically endogamous marriage are not exactly identical; the correlation coefficient (Spearman's) is .85, which suggests general similarity in the position of the nine groups over time, but which also draws attention to the fact of some displacement.

The Spanish-speaking and the French-Canadians undergo the least decline in endogamy between generations, with differences of only 8 and 11 percentage points, respectively. One explanation for this fact lies in the proximity both of these groups have to their points of emigration. Unlike the Europe-based nationalities, the Puerto Ricans, Mexicans, and Quebec French all share the facility of return visits to their areas of origin. This contributes to the maintenance of language use and ethnic attachments as well as the selection of spouses. The ease of return is enhanced by the fact that Puerto Rico, Mexico, and Canada have not historically shared the immigration restrictions imposed on European nations. Apart from the factors of geographic proximity and the absence of legal restrictions on immigration (or perhaps because of these factors), ethnic traditionalism is more characteristic of the Spanish-speaking and the French-Canadians, vis-à-vis other Catholic groups, and may persist in other forms not yet fully explored or understood. In this connection, recall the lack of educational mobility for both of these groups, and the lower occupational mobility for the French-Canadians as well, that was discussed in Chapter Two. Ethnic traditionalism, it would be expected, influences the choice of spouse as well as the avenues of socioeconomic change.

The English, too, show little loss in the proportion of endogamous marriages, but the English Catholics are the least endogamous to begin with, as well as being few in number, and the decline is not as meaningful. The Irish, the Germans, and the Italians all show similar declines, comparable to the 25 percentage point difference of the total population. The Italians, however, remain relatively endogamous (66 per cent), whereas the Irish and German Catholics are both lower than the total proportion of 55 per cent.

The greatest decline in absolute terms is that of the Lithuanians (43 points), the Eastern Europeans (47 points), and the Poles (39 points). The control of a single familial generation, built into the analysis of parental and respondent marriages, makes it all the more striking that these three groups, the majority of whom are first- or second-generation Americans, become ethnically exogamous as quickly as the data of Table 9 suggest. The reasons for this pattern will be explored in the following chapter, with a discussion of the antecedents of ethnic marriage.

The question of declining endogamy in relation to the total proportion for the national sample of Catholic Americans can be emphasized by the use of ratios. Table 10 helps to summarize this phenomenon by presenting the ratios of marriage for each ethnic group: the proportion endogamous for each background over the constant proportion endogamous for the total.

Table 10. Ratios of Ethnic Endogamous Marriage (Group Endogamy in Relation to Total Endogamy) for Respondent's and Parental Generations

Ethnicity	Respondent's Marriage	Parental Marriage	Difference
Spanish-speaking	1.60	1.20	+.40
French-Canadian	1.24	.99	+.25
Italian	1.20	1.16	+.04
Lithuanian	.91	1.16	−.25
Polish	.91	1.11	−.20
German	.82	.91	−.09
Irish	.78	.81	−.03
Eastern European	.71	1.08	−.37
English	.22	.34	−.12
Total	1.00	1.00	.00

Differences between the ratios of the respondents' and parental generations are also presented. A difference of .00, for example, would suggest no generational change in that ethnic group's marriage pattern as the pattern relates to the trend for the total Catholic population. A *plus* direction would point to endogamy patterns persisting beyond the total trend, and a *minus* direction would mean exogamy rates beyond the norm for all Catholics. Table 10 then focuses on the behavior of each ethnic group in its relationship to the total, rather than the absolute size or extent of decline of endogamy. It is a measure to control for the pattern of the total population.

From this perspective, the Spanish-speaking and the French-Canadians are considerably more endogamous in relation to other groups and the total population. The *maintenance* of their endogamous behavior is in marked contrast to the changing marital choices of other Catholic ethnic groups; this is reflected by ratio differences of +.40 for the Spanish-speaking and +.25 for the French-Canadians.

The Italians (+.04) reflect a rate of change comparable to the total Catholic population, in spite of the fact that they are still predominantly endogamous. The Irish (−.03), the Germans (−.09), and the English (−.12) show no appreciable difference from the pattern of change for all Catholics of the parental and respondents' generations.

Moving toward ethnic intermarriage within the Church at considerably faster speed, however, are the Eastern Europeans (−.37), the Lithuanians (−.25), and the Poles (−.20). As noted in discussing the absolute percentages, the effect of one family generation is strongest for these three groups. The structural factors that may help to clarify this pattern will be discussed in Chapter Four, but it is obvious at this point to anticipate the importance of the control of American generation for each ethnic group. Although the nationalities from Southern and Eastern Europe predominate among the newer immigrants, and those from Western Europe are numbered largely from the earlier periods of immigration, it will help to separate the influence of generation from ethnicity, and compare, say, the behavior of the Irish and the French-Canadians from both immigration waves, with Italian and Polish patterns from both periods. To conclude here, the expectation of increased exogamy from parents to respondents has been clearly substantiated by the data, but the rate of change from endogamy to exogamy varies considerably with the different ethnic backgrounds. The Catholic melting pot is not operating uniformly for the many different ethnic backgrounds.

CHANGING ETHNICITY: THE PATTERNS OF EXOGAMY

With the variable increase of exogamy for all groups in the Catholic population, the question of selection becomes important. When the ethnic group
does marry out of its traditional background, which other groups are chosen?
Is the process one of random selection, or does a discernible pattern emerge?
On the basis of past research into the influence of cultural factors on marriage
choice, it is expected that homogamous patterns will occur with exogamy
(Hollingshead, 1950; Thomas, 1954). That is, culturally similar groups will
tend to confine intermarriage among themselves. Table 11 shows the data for
the parental generation, relating the marriage choices of the respondents'
fathers as distributed among the respondents' mothers.

For five of the nine ethnic groups in Table 11—the Latin and Eastern
Europe nationalities—the extent of endogamy is so predominant as to preclude any appreciable out-group selection. With the Eastern European categories, there is only the slightest suggestion of ethnic exogamy among themselves; 5 per cent of the Lithuanians select Polish spouses, 4 per cent of the
Poles choose equally both German and Eastern European wives, and 6 per
cent of the Eastern bloc marry Polish women.

Among the remaining four ethnicity backgrounds, however, there is a
stronger suggestion that exogamous choices are restricted among themselves.
The French-Canadians, for example, choose the Irish (10 per cent); the Irish
select spouses from the Germans (13 per cent), the English (11 per cent), and
the French-Canadians (8 per cent); the Germans choose the Irish (12 per
cent); and the English marry the Irish (49 per cent) and the Germans (13 per
cent). Indeed, the proportion of English males choosing Irish wives is almost
twice as large (49 per cent) as the proportion they select of their own ethnic
background (27 per cent). This points clearly to the relative sizes of the
groups in the total population.

Thus far, with the data of the parental generation, there is some
suggestion of interethnic marriage being confined among the different
Eastern European origins, and there is a stronger indication of such a network among Catholics of Western European descent. Accordingly, the homogamous factors of similar generational background in the United States and
relative cultural similarities are obvious explanations.

There are two distinct problems, however, which relate to this discussion
of Table 11. The first is the question of sex-linked differences in mar-

Table 11. Per Cent Distribution of Catholic Ethnic Groups, by Ethnic Marriage Choice for Parental Generation (Respondent's Father by Respondent's Mother)

Ethnicity of Respondent's Father	Ethnicity of Respondent's Mother									
	Spanish-speaking	Italian	Lithuanian	Polish	Eastern European	French-Canadian	German	Irish	English	Total
Spanish-speaking	96	—	—	1	—	2	1	1	—	101[a] (119)
Italian	—	93	—	1	1	1	2	1	1	100 (336)
Lithuanian	—	—	93	5	2	—	—	—	—	100 (42)
Polish	—	1	1	89	4	—	4	2	1	101[a] (170)
Eastern European	—	1	—	6	86	—	4	2	—	99[a] (124)
French-Canadian	0	1	—	1	—	79	5	10	4	100 (153)
German	1	0	0	6	2	4	73	12	2	100 (234)
Irish	1	0	—	1	1	8	13	65	11	100 (269)
English	—	2	—	2	—	7	13	49	27	100 (45)
Total	8	21	3	12	8	11	16	17	4	100 (1,492)

[a] Total differs from 100 per cent because of rounding.

riage choice. Is there a difference between males and females in the patterns and rates of ethnic exogamy? Some of the literature on this subject suggests that this is a relevent factor, despite the fact that past findings are not always consistent (Haerle, 1962). This question will be examined directly in Chapter Four. The more immediate problem is whether the fathers' marriage patterns differ considerably from the mothers' behavior. Evidence previously assembled in analysis of these data indicates that there is no consistent bias in selecting the marriage choice of the fathers.[2]

The other question refers to the availability or size of the different ethnic groups in the population. The actual numbers of Catholics in ethnic groups are variable and thus may have a misleading influence on the patterns of marriage choice.[3] In an attempt to minimize this problem of relative size, ratios can be calculated in addition to percentages. These ratios are viewed as expected frequencies: the actual percentage of ethnic endogamy-exogamy for each given group, over the proportionate size of the ethnic background from which the spouse is chosen. Thus a ratio as defined will control for the availability of spouses from any given group, large or small.[4]

A ratio of 1.0 indicates the frequency of marriage expected on the basis of randomness in the population. A ratio greater than 1.0 conveys the degree of "overmarriage" with any given group, and a ratio of less than 1.0 points to the extent of "undermarriage" with any ethnicity. Both of the excessive ratios could be due to any number of factors: positive factors such as propinquitous or preferential relationships in the case of "overmarriage," and negative factors of social distance in the case of "undermarriage." The survey lacks any data that would help probe the specific influence of these kinds of attitudinal or neighborhood factors. As descriptive measures, the ratios are to be considered as gross indicators of the extent of ethnic exogamy. They account for the actual size of the ethnic group at large in the Catholic population of the United States, but they are to be qualified because they ignore the variability of fertility patterns, migration characteristics, and other important factors.

Table 12 offers the "expected" marriage ratios for the parental generation. Each ratio is the quotient of the actual proportion of wives chosen from an ethnic group over the actual percentage of females available in the same group. It is immediately apparent that each ethnic group scores its highest ratio with endogamous marriage, regardless of the size of the group.

The Lithuanians have the highest ratio of 31.0 because of two factors: they are 93 per cent endogamous in this generation, and, at the same time, they are relatively few in the total Catholic population (only 3 per cent). The Irish, on the other hand, have the lowest endogamous ratio of 3.8, because they are less endogamous (65 per cent) and more numerous among Catholic Americans (17 per cent).

Table 12. Ethnic Marriage Ratios for the Parental Generation (Actual Marriage in Relation to Proportion of Spouses)

Ethnicity of Respondent's Father	Ethnicity of Respondent's Mother								
	Spanish-speaking	Italian	Lithuanian	Polish	Eastern European	French-Canadian	German	Irish	English
Spanish-speaking	12.0	—	—	0.1	—	0.2	0.1	0.1	—
Italian	—	4.4	—	0.1	0.1	0.1	0.1	0.1	0.2
Lithuanian	—	—	31.0	0.4	0.2	—	—	—	—
Polish	—	0.0	0.3	7.4	0.5	—	0.2	0.1	0.2
Eastern European	—	0.0	—	0.5	10.8	—	0.2	0.1	—
French-Canadian	—	0.0	—	0.1	—	7.2	0.3	0.6	1.0
German	0.0	0.0	0.0	0.5	0.2	0.4	4.6	0.7	0.5
Irish	0.1	0.0	0.0	0.1	0.1	0.7	0.8	3.8	2.8
English	—	0.1	—	0.2	—	0.6	0.8	2.9	6.8

For exogamous marriages, the ratios of Table 12 are of course similar to the actual percentages of Table 11. The Spanish-speaking Catholics and the Italians are so endogamous in this generation that only negligible ratios emerge with other groups. The ratios for the Eastern European categories maintain the slight suggestion that Poles, Lithuanians, and the Eastern European bloc tend to marry among themselves when they do marry out of their respective backgrounds.

For the remaining four nationality origins, the control for the availability of spouses confirms the patterns already discussed. The French-Canadians, in exogamy, choose the English by a ratio of 1.0, or by about what might be expected by chance alone. It was shown in Table 11 that 10 per cent of the French-Canadians had Irish wives, but the Irish are so numerous in the population (especially in New England, where both groups predominate) that the figure of 10 per cent translates to a ratio of only 0.6. On the basis of regional concentrations, one might have anticipated a higher ratio of "overmarriage" between the French-Canadians and the Irish.

The Germans of this generation do not overmarry with any other group, but their ratios of exogamous marriage with other Western European groups are somewhat higher than they are with the Southern or Eastern European nationalities. The sole exception is the German-Polish ratio of 0.5.

The Irish show a ratio of 2.8 with the English, a figure considerably higher than what might be expected by random behavior. There are no other signs of preferential mating by the Irish, except for their slight tendency to marry Germans and perhaps French-Canadians, in contrast to other ethnic backgrounds.

Recall from Table 11 that a greater proportion of the English males had Irish wives than spouses of their own background. It was suggested then that this indicated the varying availability of numbers of different ethnic individuals. In Table 12, this idea is substantiated. The English have a ratio of 6.8 in endogamous marriage, and a lesser ratio of 2.9 with Irish spouses. This is explained by the true proportions of ethnic spouses in the Catholic population: only 4 per cent are English Catholics, whereas 17 per cent are Irish. For other exogamous marriages, the English do not show higher-than-chance ratios, although the tendency toward exogamy with the Germans and French-Canadians may be noted.

Although the general extent of overmarriage is not considerable, the relative arrangement of exogamy revolves around the four Western European origins. Among these Catholics of the parental generation, it is among the Irish, the English, the Germans, and the French-Canadians that some signs of marital assimilation come to the surface.

Preceding discussion showed that nearly half (45 per cent) of the contemporary Catholic population is ethnically exogamous, and it is among the respondents' own generation that clearer patterns of ethnic intermarriage may be found. Table 13 presents the distribution of ethnic marriage choice for this generation, relating the ethnic background of the respondent's father to that of the spouse's father.[5]

The strong persistence of ethnic endogamy for the Spanish-speaking Catholics disallows any significant exogamous patterns. The Spanish-speaking are 88 per cent endogamous and the interethnic choices are rather evenly, if thinly, distributed among all other Catholic ethnic groups. Endogamy for the Spanish-speaking may mean essentially any of the following, in this study: marriage among the Puerto Ricans themselves, among the Mexicans themselves, or between these groups. Because of residential concentration in different regions, most of the endogamy is no doubt strictly Mexican, or strictly Puerto Rican. Maritally, the Spanish-speaking are the most traditional and ghettoized culture in the context of American Catholicism, and this marriage pattern symbolizes the *barrio* of both Puerto Ricans and Chicanos in the pluralistic culture of the United States.

Among the remaining eight nationality backgrounds in Table 13, exogamy is more extensive, but the actual percentage distributions for these groups do not point up any particularly overwhelming patterns of ethnic choice. Selection does not relate to homogamous considerations of cultural similarity or generational background in the United States to the degree one might have anticipated.

When the Italians marry out of their own background, for example, they prefer spouses of Western European background; 10 per cent each select German and Irish Catholics. Among the Eastern European nationalities, 17 per cent of the Poles marry Germans, 11 per cent of the Lithuanians select Italians, and 13 per cent of the Eastern bloc itself chooses Germans.

There is relatively more indication of homogamy among the choices of the French-Canadians, Germans, and Irish. The larger proportions are indeed limited to their own pool. The English, however, do not limit ethnic selection to the other Western nationalities: although 30 per cent of the English choose Irish spouses, and another 12 per cent marry Germans, the data show that the English also select Eastern Europeans (15 per cent) and Italians (12 per cent).

As noted with the parental generation, the availability of the numbers of ethnic individuals is important. Another appraisal of exogamous choice can be given with marriage ratios, based on the sizes of the different ethnic groups in the population. Again, it is important to qualify these indicators of marriage choice inasmuch as this random-chance model is limited by the extent to which ethnic groups are distributed unevenly in the population. Table 14 presents the ratios of actual marriage behavior given the proportions of the ethnic backgrounds in the society.

Table 13. Per Cent Distribution of Catholic Ethnic Groups, by Ethnic Marriage Choice for Respondent's Generation (Respondent's Father by Spouse's Father)

Ethnicity of Respondent's Father	Ethnicity of Spouse's Father									
	Spanish-speaking	Italian	Lithuanian	Polish	Eastern European	French-Canadian	German	Irish	English	Total
Spanish-speaking	88	2	—	1	2	1	1	2	2	99ª (88)
Italian	1	66	1	3	3	2	10	10	4	100 (256)
Lithuanian	—	11	50	11	8	3	8	5	5	101ª (38)
Polish	2	10	2	50	8	4	17	5	1	99ª (135)
Eastern European	1	13	1	11	39	3	13	11	8	100 (90)
French-Canadian	1	3	1	3	2	68	9	10	3	100 (112)
German	1	4	—	10	7	3	45	20	11	101ª (165)
Irish	1	9	1	4	3	8	16	43	15	100 (179)
English	—	12	—	8	15	12	12	30	12	101ª (27)
Total	8	21	3	11	7	10	16	16	7	99ª (1,090)

ª Total differs from 100 per cent because of rounding.

Table 14. Ethnic Marriage Ratios for the Respondent's Generation (Actual Marriage in Relation to Proportion of Spouses)

Ethnicity of Respondent's Father	Ethnicity of Spouse's Father								
	Spanish-speaking	Italian	Lithuanian	Polish	Eastern European	French-Canadian	German	Irish	English
Spanish-speaking	11.0	0.1	—	0.1	0.3	0.1	0.1	0.1	0.3
Italian	0.1	3.1	0.3	0.3	0.4	0.2	0.6	0.6	0.6
Lithuanian	—	0.5	16.7	1.0	1.1	0.3	0.5	0.3	0.7
Polish	0.2	0.5	0.7	4.5	1.1	0.4	1.1	0.3	0.1
Eastern European	0.1	0.6	0.3	1.0	5.6	0.3	0.8	0.7	1.1
French-Canadian	0.1	0.1	0.3	0.3	0.3	6.8	0.6	0.6	0.4
German	0.1	0.2	—	0.9	1.0	0.3	2.8	1.2	1.6
Irish	0.1	0.4	0.3	0.4	0.4	0.8	1.0	2.7	2.1
English	—	0.6	—	0.7	2.1	1.2	0.8	1.9	1.7

As with the parental generation, contemporary Lithuanians have the highest ratio, this time of 16.7, because of their small size in the Catholic population. The English, on the other hand, have the lowest endogamous ratio (1.7) because of their infrequent in-group marriage. In fact, the English have a higher marriage ratio with the Irish (1.9) and the Eastern Europeans (2.1) than they have with themselves. Whether this is necessarily prophetic for the future marital assimilation of the other ethnic groups, it is not possible to say. It *is* strong evidence, however, of the loss of English Catholic ethnicity, and it is not at all surprising inasmuch as the English Catholics are distributed throughout all regions of the United States and have no particular concentration in either urban or rural settlements. In contrast, all other groups still persist in scoring higher ratios with endogamous marriage than in any form of exogamy.

Although not conclusive, certain facts can be drawn from the data of Table 14. Three groups of this contemporary generation persist in ethnic endogamy and at the same time avoid overmarriage with any other ethnic backgrounds: the Spanish-speaking, the Italians, and the French-Canadians all share this characteristic. None of these groups marries into other ethnic cultures at the level one might expect on the basis of chance alone. Their marriages with different groups do not reflect any preferential pattern but are instead distributed thinly among all groups.

The three backgrounds from Eastern Europe do not display the homogamous behavior one might expect from the suggestion of their parents' marriage choices. For the contemporary Catholics, the Lithuanians select Poles and Eastern Europeans as spouses only at the level one might expect on the basis of chance. The Polish Catholics themselves select spouses who are of other Eastern European background at the same ratio as they select German Catholics. And the Eastern European bloc is just as likely to marry the English as they are the Poles.

More homogamy is evident among the Germans, the Irish, and the English, with the exception that both the Germans and the English tend to select Eastern Europeans as spouses, either at the level one might expect by chance or even higher.

In general, the higher marriage ratios tend to cluster around the endogamous ratio for each group presented in Table 14 (observing that the listing of ethnicities is offered in the following order: the two Latin groups, the three Eastern European categories, and the four nationalities of Western European or Canadian origin). The levels of the ratios and the exceptions to this pattern, however, suggest modifications of the expectations of homogamy: ethnic groups of similar immigration periods or of similar European region or culture will necessarily intermarry when they do leave their own background.

The Spanish-speaking, the Italians, and the French-Canadians all maintain in this generation viable endogamous behavior. Not only do all three groups show a distinct majority in the proportions marrying within their respective groups, but they all avoid any signs of overmarriage with or preference for other ethnic backgrounds when exogamy does take place. The 12 per cent of the Spanish-speaking, the 32 per cent of the French-Canadians, and the 34 per cent of the Italians who do marry out of their groups do not demonstrate any proclivity toward marriage with any particular group. Their interethnic marriages are random, as well as few in number.

SUMMARY

At this point, it is safe to conclude that all of the commonplace expectations of widespread intermarriage among American ethnic groups, even with the limitation of marriage within a shared religion, simply have not yet materialized. The Catholic melting pot is not a reality for all the many ethnic constituent parts. To be sure, there are tendencies toward, and evidence of increases in, ethnic exogamy between generations, but the most important finding is the variability of this kind of assimilation.

The Mexicans, the Puerto Ricans, the French-Canadians, and the Italians are not disappearing into the greater body of American Catholicism. They are marrying into their own groups, at the rate of better than six out of every ten. But even more surprisingly, the present-day Irish and German Catholics, whose families have been in the United States for three or more generations, maintain endogamous marriages by proportions of more than 40 per cent, and when the Irish and Germans do marry out, they marry into generationally similar Western European backgrounds.

There is another curious pattern that emerges from the findings of this chapter. One would expect, at least on the basis of Catholic melting pot speculation, that the three groups which are the largest Catholic ethnic groups from the northeast regions of the country would show higher-than-chance marriage among themselves. Yet there are few marriages between the Irish and the Italians (ratios of 0.4 and 0.6), between the Irish and the Poles (ratios of 0.4 and 0.3), and between the Italians and the Poles (ratios of 0.3 and 0.5). One can grant that each group tends to predominate in a different region (the Irish in New England, the Italians in the Middle Atlantic states, and the Poles in East North Central), but they are the three largest Catholic groups in size and the three most urban in these regions, and each is not unrepresented where the other two frequently live. Yet there are no overall indicators to their getting together in religioethnic assimilation.

Given the essential meaning of cultural variety when we talk about different ethnic backgrounds, it should not be too surprising to find that ethnicity still serves as a cultural force in affecting rates of change and persists as a foundation of diversity. The surprise lies more in our overestimation of the impact of the larger American society on traditional ethnic ways. The next chapter probes the factors in American society that are expected to influence the choice of marriage, to clarify the foregoing findings and contribute further to our understanding of the meaning of pluralism.

NOTES

1. Since the study emphasis is on the patterning of ethnic endogamy and exogamy *within* Catholicism (either within or across nationality lines, but always intrareligious), certain basic exclusions are necessary. Thus the cases that refer to respondents with non-Catholic fathers and mothers (to include here the presently converted Catholics) are omitted from the analysis. For the parental generation, endogamous couples number 1194 and exogamous couples total 298.

    The numbers of cases for the marriages of the respondent's generation are 600 endogamous couples and 490 exogamous couples. In addition to exclusions made for the parental generation, the natural exclusions here include all born-Catholics who are not married presently or who have non-Catholic spouses.

    For determining whether the ethnicity of a couple is similar or dissimilar, an examination was made of the respondent's father's main nationality and the spouse's father's main nationality. If they are reported as the same, the couple is considered to represent an endogamous marriage. If they report different nationalities, the couple is defined as an exogamous marriage. The same procedure was taken for the parental marriage, considering the nationality backgrounds reported for one's father and one's mother.

    The father's background is chosen in preference to the mother's, in analysis reported in this book, for reasons of the family name and the ethnic identity which is presumed to adhere to the surname, as well as to facilitate comparison with previous research using the same method. This arbitrary decision remains to be tested as the "better" indicator of ethnic group membership; it is not meant to deny the relevance of the mother's role in ethnic behavior.

    A question on religious status offers data on whether the respondent is a born Catholic or a convert. The question asking for the religion of the spouse is limited to current religious preference (Catholic or other); no information is available on the religion in which the spouse was raised. For more information on the questions of the survey, and for a copy of the interview schedule, see Greeley and Rossi (1966).

A discussion on the theoretical qualifications of the concepts of endogamy and exogamy is presented in Chapter Seven, along with an analysis of the consequences of both kinds of marriage for the religious behavior of Catholic Americans.

2. Proportions of ethnic endogamy in the parental generation may be calculated in each of the four different combinations: respondent's father's choice of respondent's mother; respondent's mother's choice of respondent's father; spouse's father's choice of spouse's mother; and spouse's mother's choice of spouse's father. These were compared and analyzed, and no bias was observed; the rank orders and sizes of the proportions of ethnic endogamy are nearly identical. See Abramson (1969, p. 231).

3. A related problem is the extent of ethnic concentration in geographical regions and specific locations, as shown in Chapter Two. Regional analysis is offered in Chapter Four, along with other demographic factors antecedent in time to the act of marriage.

4. I wish to acknowledge the assistance of Seymour Sudman, of the staff of the National Opinion Research Center, University of Chicago, where this survey was conducted, in the preparation of the ethnic endogamy and exogamy ratios.

5. As noted above in note 2 for the parental generation, the same analysis was made of the different combinations yielding proportions of ethnic endogamy. Eight different combinations were calculated for the respondent's generation, and rank orders and sizes of proportions are found to be very similar; no bias was detected in selecting the patterns of the respondent's father's relationship to the spouse's father. See Abramson (1969, p. 232).

CHAPTER FOUR

ANTECEDENTS OF ETHNIC MARRIAGE

European immigrants to America, sharing sufficiently common institutions of kinship and marriage and recognizing American common law as the appropriate standard to regulate these relations, are subject to no national proscriptions against intermarriage. Such groups are, however, influenced by their own collective regulations and by accidents of circumstance, locations, and the order in which they entered American society.

M. G. SMITH (1969)

MUCH OF THE PRECEDING INVESTIGATION of diversity has pointed to the immediate relevance of specific sociological variables. The association of ethnic concentrations with geographical regions in the United States, for example, raises the question of the propinquity factor. The interwoven quality of ethnicity itself with a distinct period of immigration history draws attention to the need for a direct look at the influence of generation. The level of education, as an indicator of social class and status, is crucial for the Americanization thesis of social change.

These and other factors are the subject of this chapter: what generates ethnic exogamy among Catholic Americans? What factors can be said to contribute to the persistence of endogamy within each of the Catholic ethnic groups? What are the causes of exogamous behavior and the marital dissolution of the ethnic communities? And further, what factors, societal and religious, can be said to have universal influence on ethnic marriage patterns, and what are the exceptions to the patterns found?

Seven specific societal factors are examined: region of the United States, size of hometown, generation in the society, sex, age, socioeconomic background, and level of education. These are followed by a discussion of the type of schooling (public or parochial) and the religious background of the parental home. The analysis in every case relates the influence of these factors to the respondent himself and his own endogamous or exogamous marriage.

REGIONAL INFLUENCE

In accord with the literature and research that has explored patterns of intermarriage in specifically defined locations, the most analogous expectation to be drawn here is the propinquity hypothesis: Intermarriage by any given group tends to be more prevalent in those areas where that group is smaller in size and less proportionate in the total population (Kennedy, 1943; Schnepp and Roberts, 1952). It is reasonable to expect more exogamy where the number of available spouses from any given background is relatively scarce.

Table 15 presents two sets of information: the type of ethnic marriage and the percentage of Catholic population, both for each region.[1] As given in the bottom row of the table, the proportion Catholic in each region declines from a high of nearly half in the six states of New England to a low of 10 per cent in the combined three subregions of the South. The proportion then rises to nearly 20 per cent in the Mountain and Pacific states of the West. The progression mirrors the immigration settlement patterns discussed in Chapter Two; the higher proportions are in the states north of the Mason-Dixon line and east of the Mississippi River.

Now consider the distribution of the type of ethnic marriage offered by region in Table 15. It is important to recall that all these marriages are religiously homogeneous. The respondents are all born Catholic with Catholic parents, and current spouses are all Catholic in religious preference. The heterogeneous quality of the exogamy is ethnic, not religious. Yet the proportion

Table 15. Type of Ethnic Marriage and Percentage Catholic Population, by Region of the United States

Type of Ethnic Marriage	Region of the United States						
	New England	Middle Atlantic	East North Central	West North Central	South	West	
Endogamy	62	59	45	43	42	64	
Exogamy	38	41	55	57	58	36	
Total	100	100	100	100	100	100	
	(175)	(402)	(256)	(93)	(43)	(128)	$N = 1,097^a$
Percentage Catholic population[b]	48.05	35.95	25.91	19.95	10.35	19.38	

[a] The total N of 1097 represents the working case total for all tables in this chapter. It is the sum of all born Catholics who have both Catholic parents and Catholic spouses, as follows:

$$N = 1,097$$
Converts, NA converts =	252
Non-Catholic parents =	244
Not married =	190
Non-Catholic spouses =	175
NAP ethnicity =	113

$$\text{Total} = 2,071$$

[b] The data providing the percentages of Catholic population by region are for 1964, the year of the survey. For the total U.S. population: U.S. Bureau of the Census, 1964. For estimated figures on the Catholic population: *Official Catholic Directory*, 1964.

Table 16.   Per Cent Exogamous, by Ethnicity and Region of the United States

Ethnicity	Region of the United States			
	New England	Middle Atlantic	North Central	South and West
German	100	75	45	69
	(1)[a]	(36)	(99)	(29)
Polish	86	48	46	62
	(7)[a]	(44)	(71)	(13)
Irish	49	47	77	61
	(45)	(68)	(43)	(23)
Eastern European	47	47	74	60
	(19)	(53)	(46)	(10)
Italian	46	27	49	38
	(24)	(163)	(45)	(24)
Spanish-speaking	33	5	43	8
	(3)[a]	(19)	(7)[a]	(59)
French-Canadian	14	60	61	60
	(69)	(5)[a]	(28)	(10)
Total	38	41	56	42
	(175)	(402)	(349)	(171)

$$N = 1,097$$

[a] Too few cases for adequate percentaging.

of endogamous marriages correlates positively with the proportion of Catholics in the regional populations.

Ethnic endogamy is highest in New England at 62 per cent of all marriages. Endogamy follows the regional trail west and south, declining to 42 per cent in the South. The proportion endogamous rises again to 64 per cent in the West. What is implicit here is the influence of the ethnic factor or concentration within each region, as detailed in Chapter Two. Under normally random ethnic proportions within each geographical location, one would not expect any correlation between the proportion of ethnic endogamy and the proportion Catholic in the total population. But under conditions where the highest proportions of total Catholics in regions mean high percentages of a given specific ethnicity as well, the analysis leads directly to the distribution of particular ethnic rates of endogamy and exogamy in each region. What is the behavior of a given group which is concentrated in a region, say, with a lower proportion of Catholic residents? Table 16 provides the answer.

The percentage exogamous for each ethnic group, as shown in Table 16, tends to be lowest in that region in which the group predominates, regardless of the size of the region or the total proportion of Catholics there. The Irish and the French-Canadians are concentrated in New England, and it is this region where Irish endogamy persists and French-Canadian endogamy flourishes. Only 49 per cent of the Irish and a mere 14 per cent of the French-Canadians in New England intermarry. The Irish, also numerous in the Middle Atlantic states, have only 47 per cent intermarrying there. In other regions, the proportion exogamous rises for both the Irish and the French-Canadians.

The same pattern obtains for each of the other groups in Table 16. German exogamy is least prevalent in the North Central region (presumably the western half), and Polish exogamy is least frequent in the same region (presumably the eastern half). The Middle Atlantic states of New York, New Jersey, and Pennsylvania are where the Italians and Eastern Europeans predominate, and it is here that these groups are most endogamous. There is also the strong suggestion, but with the problem of very few cases in other regions, that the Mexican Catholics are endogamous in the West and the Puerto Ricans in the Middle Atlantic, again where these groups have enclaves.

It would, of course, be advantageous to confront this question of propinquity more directly, as a relationship, say, of the size of the local ethnic community and the percentage of endogamy and exogamy associated with that community. The data in this study do not include questions that measure the extent of the ethnic community of which the Catholic respondent is a local member. As a result, there is a necessary dependence on the larger influence of the region, as a kind of gross indicator of communality. The fact that the relationship emerges at this broader level is important for the study of regionalism in America, as well as for the prospects of the study of the persisting and changing ethnic community within the nation's regions.

RURAL-URBAN DIFFERENCES

Another factor already shown to be relevant for the extent of diversity within American Catholicism is the size of the hometown. As with the foregoing discussion of the influence of regionalism, I am not able to control for the size of the actual ethnic community with these data in the subsequent analysis. The relationship is limited to the impact of rural and urban background on ethnic marriage behavior, for the present with no controls.

One might expect that intermarriage, whether ethnic or religious, would increase with the size of the hometown because of increased opportunities for meeting and marrying individuals from different ethnic or religious backgrounds in settlements of greater population. On the other hand, one might also suppose that there could be more endogamy in urban areas by virtue of the larger and more viable ethnic neighborhoods, which are typically part of larger cities.

The data from this survey confirm the former expectation (Abramson, 1969, p. 86). The correlation is clearly positive; only one-third of the Catholics raised on farms and in the open countryside marry into different ethnic backgrounds, as compared with one-half of the urban dwellers who do so. Ethnic endogamy then is partly a function of rural American background. The relative isolation of small towns, no larger than 10,000 in population, and the greater isolation of farming environments contribute to the marital unity of the ethnic group (studies of language-maintenance also cite the rural persistence of ethnicity, e.g., Nelson, 1948; Haugen, 1953; Fishman, 1966; Lieberson, 1970).

There may be specific ethnic differentiation in this relationship, inasmuch as the Spanish-speaking, for example, are so highly endogamous *and* of rural background. A control for the ethnic factor would be important. Table 17 offers the percentage exogamous by size of hometown and ethnic background.

Table 17. Per Cent Exogamous, by Ethnicity and Size of Hometown

	Size of Hometown	
Ethnicity	Rural Area	Urban Area
Polish	58	47
	(36)	(95)
Irish	52	57
	(44)	(134)
German	46	71
	(96)	(69)
Eastern European	45	69
	(60)	(68)
Italian	32	35
	(98)	(158)
French-Canadian	25	36
	(40)	(72)
Spanish-speaking	5	22
	(56)	(32)
Total	38	50
	(445)	(647)

$$N = 1,092$$
$$\text{NA hometown} = 5$$
$$\text{Total} = 1,097$$

For the most part, the influence of hometown size is constant in the same direction; exogamy is more often associated with urban background. The Eastern Europeans and the Germans are the most influenced by this factor, and the Italians and the Irish are the least so. The Spanish-speaking, predominantly rural and endogamous, also conform to this pattern; only 5 per cent of the rural Spanish-speaking marry other Catholics, in contrast to the 22 per cent of the urban Mexicans and Puerto Ricans who do.

The one exception to the pattern revealed in Table 17 are the Polish Catholics. Curiously, they show the reverse behavior. For the Poles, it is rural life which is more associated with ethnic change; 58 per cent of the Poles raised in small towns and on farms have become exogamous, in contrast to the 47 per cent of the Poles raised in urban areas. Indeed, the rural Poles are even more exogamous than the rural Irish and Germans.

Although the significance of this difference may well be qualified, the Polish exception poses a challenge to the generalization that larger cities, because of their more diverse and cosmopolitan populations, tend to encourage interethnic contact and marital assimilation. For the Poles, the urban environment affords more opportunity to *sustain* an endogamous community, perhaps because of specifically ethnic institutions. It is difficult at this point to understand just why this may be so for the Polish Catholics but not for the others discussed. Part of the explanation may be ethnodemographic; the rural Poles might lack the numbers of individuals in local settlements and this sparse rural community might therefore inhibit endogamy. There may also be a generational or nativity difference between urban and rural Polish communities. This idea is pursued in the following section.

GENERATION IN THE UNITED STATES

As much of the book has indicated thus far, those ethnic groups whose members' families have resided in the United States for several generations or longer are clearly more likely to be ethnically exogamous than those whose immigration experiences have been more recent. It is not possible to learn from this survey what proportion of the first-generation foreign-born Catholics were married abroad in their countries of origin. Of the total sample 10 per cent were born abroad, and those who emigrated as adults may well have brought (endogamous) spouses with them.

The more crucial question at this stage is the extent to which the pattern of generational influence on intermarriage is true for given nationality backgrounds. One might easily expect on the basis of cumulative cultural assimilation over generations that the influence of nativity would be considerably greater than ethnic background per se. For the total Catholic population, the proportion exogamous rises with generation; the first generation is only 23 per cent intermarried, the second is 42 per cent, and the third or later is 58 per cent (Abramson, 1969, p. 90). Is this model characteristic of all Catholic groups?

Table 18 details the degree of generational influence. For five of the seven groups shown, the pattern is as expected. It is particularly true for the French-Canadians (an endogamous 21 per cent of the newer generations, as compared with 50 per cent of the older generations) and the Italians (with twice as many of the older generations intermarrying). For the Spanish-speaking, there is no apparent generational difference. The Mexicans and the Puerto Ricans, however, are almost exclusively first and second generation, and the case base for the older generations, is too small for any significant

Table 18.   Per Cent Exogamous, by Ethnicity and Generation in the United States

	Generation in the United States	
Ethnicity	Newer Generation (first and second)	Older Generation (third and later)
German	65 (57)	52 (99)
Eastern European	56 (108)	72 (18)
Polish	47 (93)	59 (37)
Irish	45 (55)	61 (120)
Italian	29 (215)	58 (38)
French-Canadian	21 (62)	50 (40)
Spanish-speaking	12 (78)	11 (9)[a]
Total	38 (678)	58 (382)

$$N = 1,060$$
$$\text{DK generation} = 36$$
$$\text{NA generation} = 1$$

$$\text{Total} = 1,097$$

[a] Too few cases for adequate percentaging.

conclusion here. In his study of Puerto Ricans in New York, however, Joseph Fitzpatrick (1966) found evidence of significant increase in exogamy among second-generation Puerto Ricans on the mainland (although there is no information on the ethnic backgrounds involved in the out-group marriages); the increase between first- and second-generation Puerto Ricans in 1949–1959 was as great as the increase reported by Drachsler (1921) for all immigrants in New York in 1908–1912. The same pattern of increasing generational exogamy is found among the Mexicans of Los Angeles County (Mittelbach and Moore, 1968; Grebler, Moore, and Guzman, 1970).

The one ethnic group that does show a reverse pattern is the German Catholic; 65 per cent of the newer generations intermarry (the highest percentage of all first- and second-generation Catholics), but only 52 per cent of the older generation Germans are exogamous. Even the older generations from Southern and Eastern Europe show more exogamy than their German counterparts.

Since many of the German Catholics are of rural background, a control for the size of hometown might help to explain this finding. Table 19 presents the relationship between ethnic marriage and generational background,

Table 19. Per Cent Exogamous, by Ethnicity, Generation in the United States, and Size of Hometown

Ethnicity	Newer Generation		Older Generation	
	Rural	Urban	Rural	Urban
German	65	64	34	74
	(34)	(25)	(56)	(43)
Polish	48	46	69	56
	(21)	(68)	(13)	(25)
Irish	31	51	63	60
	(16)	(39)	(27)	(92)
Italian	28	29	50	64
	(82)	(133)	(16)	(22)
French-Canadian	17	22	38	56
	(23)	(40)	(13)	(27)
Total	33	41	46	65
	(280)	(398)	(149)	(233)

$$N = 1,060$$
DK generation =   31
NA generation =   1
NA hometown =   5

Total = 1,097

controlling for rural-urban origins, for five selected ethnic groups. The total figures in Table 19 pertain to all marriages and reflect the combined influence of hometown background and length of residence in the United States. The percentage exogamous steadily increases from a low of 33 per cent of the newer generations brought up in small towns and rural areas to a high of 65 per cent of the older generations raised in urban centers.

One might have expected that the urban influence would work for both generations of German Catholics. Instead, size of hometown actually makes no difference among the more recent German Americans; whether of rural or urban background, German Catholics of the first and second generation are still the most likely of all ethnics to intermarry. Size of hometown does affect the older generation Germans, however; whereas only 34 per cent of the rural older generation intermarries, as many as 74 per cent of the urban older generation are exogamous. The difference is considerable, for the 34 per cent figure is the lowest of all rural Catholics of the older generations, and the 74 per cent is the highest proportion for all older generations in the cities.

There are two striking facts to be explained. The first is the excessive inclination of German Catholics of the first and second generations to marry non-Germans, even more eagerly than would be indicated by the "normative" behavior of the total sample of Catholic Americans. The second fact to be emphasized is the persistence of the older generation Germans, raised in small towns and rural areas, to remain endogamous, again in marked contrast to the marital behavior of all other groups.

With regard to the larger subcultural and subsocietal nature of the German community in America, the historian John Hawgood (1940) has drawn an extended and generalized picture which offers some clues to this behavior. Hawgood has argued that this group (both Protestant and Catholic) was more "German" than "American" during the later nineteenth and early twentieth century, and that it was the impact of World War I that destroyed the hyphenated quality of their culture and served to bring about fuller assimilation into the larger society. Without any specific references to the condition of German endogamy, Hawgood demonstrated that the war and the anti-German feelings it engendered within the United States helped to break down the cohesiveness of the German community and to thwart the maintenance of German American institutions and organizations.

Although there are alternative interpretations of the nature of the German immigrant's political allegiance and value system during this period of adjustment, most writers seem to agree on the social-psychological effect of America's wars on the German community (Kloss, 1966; Gleason, 1968, pp. 144–171). With regard to language use, for example, Joshua Fishman and

John Hofman (1966, p. 40) explained in their empirical analysis of language maintenance: "Certainly, the drop in 1920 of second-generation claimants of German mother tongue must be attributed in part to anti-German sentiments fostered by World War I." Their research also documents the sharp loss in the number of second-generation claimants of the German language in the years between 1940 and 1960, a result of the domestic impact of World War II.

Although this survey does not include any information on the use of foreign languages by Catholic Americans, it does not seem unreasonable to assume an association between the claim of some knowledge of the ethnic tongue and the conditions of ethnic endogamy. Both would be positive measures of ethnic cohesiveness and cultural continuity. If political events such as conflicts between adopted country and motherland appear to influence the language maintenance of a group, they might be expected to bear upon the extent of ethnic endogamy as well.

More of the study of language use among German Americans is analogous to the study of endogamy. The erosion of the maintenance of the German tongue, as Heinz Kloss (1966, pp. 232–233) points out, was not always a clear path of assimilation from German culture to American mores:

What may well have constituted one of the greatest handicaps of the German Americans was, at that time, generally considered to be a decided asset, namely, the continual reinforcement from new waves of immigrants. Quantitatively, the newcomers meant a strengthening of the ranks. But, at the same time, they prevented the earlier arrivals and their children and grandchildren from consolidating their gains, from assuming a set attitude, from acquiring an outspoken and specifically German-American (i.e., neither European-German nor Anglo-American) outlook of their own. The newcomers both served as a crutch and undermined the self-reliance of the old stock by driving home to them that their language was tainted with Anglicisms, their acquaintance with the latest developments in literary German defective, and their way of life devoid of higher graces. . . . The newcomers kept alive among many American-born German Americans a feeling that the German language was somehow bound up with foreigners and with foreignness, something not entirely rooted in New World soil. It is, therefore, no accident that the persistence of the language was greatest in those sections, where, since the 1890's, the number of recent immigrants remained comparatively small, such as Texas and certain parts of rural Wisconsin and Minnesota.

In addition to the psychological and cultural conflicts represented here between the older and newer generations, the style of German ethnicity in the United States is further complicated by the tensions of the two World Wars. It would not be surprising, given these circumstances, to learn that the historically strong ethnic consciousness of German Americans would come to be the preserve of the older generations who had settled in rural and isolated areas of the Middle West. It is as though the waves of change of twentieth-century America swept over the Germans of the United States, leaving only the earliest immigrants in the rural backwater untouched.

The newer generations of German Americans were more conscious of the social and political tensions between Germany and the United States, and at the same time, embarrassed by the so-called crude attempts of the earlier generations to maintain *Kultur*. [For other groups, notably the Jews, the arrival of the newer immigrants from Eastern Europe also triggered degrees of embarrassment, but the embarrassment became the property of the earlier arriving German Jews; the sense of cultural dissonance resulted, however, in the same increased desire and search for American assimilation (Rischin, 1962, pp. 95–111).]

Compared with the older generation Germans in the rural areas, Germans of third and later generation in the cities were more vulnerable to anti-German propaganda and the hostile atmosphere surrounding everything German that first developed during the years of World War I, as well as being more vulnerable to the criticism of their more recently arrived fellow Germans. Given this background, ethnic cohesion began to wear away, and assimilation in the form of ethnic exogamy and the abandonment of the German language took hold.

In contrast to their coreligionists, the Polish Catholics display the opposite behavior. As Table 19 also indicated, it is the Poles of older generations and rural background who are the *most* exogamous (69 per cent) instead of the least. Urban Poles of the older generations apparently are more influenced by the conditions of the urban environment, and presumably the vitality of the Polish community within the city, than they are by the fact of being long resident in the United States. Their exogamous behavior is not much different from that of Polish Catholics who are either immigrants or the children of immigrants, among whom rural or urban background makes no difference at all.

Perhaps it is simply that, lacking the ethnic visibility of a fairly large community with its particularly ethnic institutions (the press, parochial schools, local organizations), such as those of the Polish quarters of Buffalo, Cleveland, Chicago, or Milwaukee, Poles in rural areas respond more to the assimilating forces of being several generations in the United States. Or, as the data of Table 19 also suggest, the numbers of older generation Polish Catholics in rural areas (there are fewer cases in the parentheses for this category) may be simply too few to sustain any thriving endogamous community. What is required then is not merely a control for size of town but also the size of the local ethnic group. The shortage of concrete sociological research in this area of ethnic change and persistence raises many questions which for the time being are difficult to answer.

In addition to pointing out the peculiarly ethnic behavior of the German and Polish Catholics, Table 19 shows the considerable influence that both generation and size of hometown play in the life of the French-Canadians. From a low of 17 per cent among the rural first- and second-generation French-Canadians, the percentage exogamous climbs to a high of 56 among the older generations who were raised in the cities. For no other group do *both* factors of generation and size of settlement have such a large impact on marriage choice. The Irish and the Italians show similar patterns of change, except that the size of hometown makes no difference among the older generation Irish or among the newer generation Italians.

SEX AND AGE AS CORRELATES OF EXOGAMY

Past research into the antecedents of intermarriage has shown the fairly mixed associations that exogamy is likely to have with the factor of sex (Haerle, 1962). Although differences have often varied, it is frequently hypothesized that males are more likely to select spouses from other backgrounds because of the greater freedom American society has typically offered males in matters of courtship and mate selection. Under general normative constraints (especially ethnic ones), it is argued, females in the United States are more likely to adopt traditional roles and be passive in courtship, which tends to leave the females more endogamous in the groups into which they were born.

The assembled data of this survey, however, offer no strong confirmation of this expectation (Abramson, 1969, p. 98). The difference for the total numbers of Catholic marriages is only 5 per cent, although the direction for greater ethnic exogamy is toward the males. The Irish, the Eastern Europeans, the Germans, and the Italians all show males to be somewhat more exogamous than females, but the differences are not appreciable. The Poles and the Spanish-speaking reveal virtually no difference, and the French-Canadians offer a 7 per cent difference favoring the females. At this level, the ethnic control does not produce any serious findings, and the differences between the sexes are not large enough to create any problems of bias.

The influence of age, on the other hand, is fairly strong. There is a steady rise in the percentage exogamous as the age of the respondent decreases; those in their fifties are 35 per cent exogamous, in their forties 44 per cent, in their thirties 48 per cent, and the youngest in their twenties are 55 per cent exogamous (Abramson, 1969, p. 99). The older Catholics, those

Table 20.   Per Cent Exogamous, by Ethnicity and Age of Respondent

Ethnicity	Age of Respondent	
	Twenties to Thirties	Forties to Fifties
Eastern European	70	50
	(47)	(80)
German	64	50
	(74)	(90)
Polish	58	44
	(55)	(79)
Irish	55	59
	(98)	(79)
Italian	42	27
	(106)	(150)
French-Canadian	32	33
	(60)	(52)
Spanish-speaking	14	6
	(56)	(32)
Total	50	41
	(516)	(575)

$$N = 1,091$$
$$\text{NA age} = 6$$
$$\text{Total} = 1,097$$

who are in their forties and fifties, are of course that much closer to the experiences of immigration and their respective ethnic cultures, either personally or generationally, and their marriages reflect this fact.

When controlling for ethnicity (Table 20,) there is some evidence of different behavior. All of the nationalities, with the exception of two, show the pattern just described. The younger members are considerably more exogamous than the older, despite the actual range or level of intermarriage. The Eastern European (comprising all nationality backgrounds from Eastern Europe except for the Polish and Lithuanian Catholics) emerge as the most exogamous in the younger age category. The two exceptions to the pattern are the Irish and the French-Canadians; the younger members of these two groups are clearly no more exogamous than the older Irish and French-Canadian Catholics. If generation in the United States has the influence it was shown to have for these two ethnic groups (in Table 18), then why should the factor of the respondent's age weaken the association with exogamy? It would seem reasonable to expect to find the influence of some factor, operating among the younger Irish and French-Canadians, which serves to retard the process of ethnic mingling and maintain the unity of the group. The involvement of the Irish and the French-Canadian Catholics in the parochial school system may explain this finding, and this will be investigated shortly.

SOCIOECONOMIC STATUS BACKGROUND

Before looking into the specific relationships of the level and type of education and the kind of ethnic marriage, it is important to consider the more generalized socioeconomic background in which the respondent was raised. One would expect, on the basis that higher status increases the number of opportunities one has in meeting individuals from different backgrounds, to find a positive correlation between status and ethnic exogamy. Table 21 examines the association between parental status (as measured by Duncan's socioeconomic scale for occupations)[2] and the type of respondent's marriage, with a control for ethnicity.

Table 21 shows some class influence for the total undifferentiated Catholic population; whereas half of those Catholics from higher status back-

Table 21. Per Cent Exogamous, by Ethnicity and Parental Socioeconomic Status (Duncan Occupational Scale)

Ethnicity	Parental Socioeconomic Status	
	Low (1–2)	High (3–10)
Eastern European	59	57
	(88)	(37)
Irish	57	55
	(61)	(111)
German	48	68
	(92)	(65)
Polish	48	54
	(75)	(51)
Italian	34	32
	(126)	(125)
French-Canadian	25	43
	(61)	(40)
Spanish-speaking	9	21
	(68)	(19)
Total	41	50
	(599)	(488)

$$N = 1,087$$
NA father's occupation $= \quad 10$

Total $= 1,097$

Table 22.   Per Cent Exogamous, by Parental Socioeconomic Status, Generation in the United States, and Size of Hometown

Generation in the United States	Size of Hometown	Parental Socioeconomic Status	
		Low (1–2)	High (3–10)
Older generation (third and later)	Urban	64 (80)	66 (151)
	Rural	40 (97)	56 (52)
Newer generation (first and second)	Urban	40 (212)	43 (181)
	Rural	33 (193)	33 (84)

$$N = 1,050$$
DK generation = 31
NA generation = 1
NA father's occupation = 10
NA hometown = 5

Total = 1,097

grounds became exogamous, only 41 per cent of those from lower status families did so. The difference is not large, and only three of the seven groups shown reveal any association. The Germans, the French-Canadians, and the Spanish-speaking are the only nationality backgrounds to have considerable differences, associating exogamy with higher socioeconomic background. Fishman and his colleagues (1966) have called these three groups the major regional language islands of the United States. Perhaps the persistence of the native tongue and the relative displacement by the English language correlate with socioeconomic background. This cannot be tested here, but among these three groups higher status may be a function of knowledge of English or at least bilingualism. In this case, ethnic exogamy and associations with Catholics of different nationality backgrounds outside the sphere of the mother tongue would measurably increase among those whose language was not limited to or prescribed by that of the traditional ethnic community.

Generally, then, parental socioeconomic status has limited influence on ethnic marriage. In contrast to the effect of generation in the United States and the size of settlement, social class origins are not as crucial as anticipated. Another way of examining the relative impact of class together with generation and hometown background is provided by Table 22, for all Catholic marriages in the United States.

Table 22 shows that the three societal factors have an additive effect on ethnic exogamy. The proportions of intermarriage increase, reading up the table from left column to right. As conditions change from newer generation to older, from rural background to urban, and from lower class origins to higher, the proportion of ethnic exogamy doubles from 33 to 66 per cent.

Social class background clearly has the least effect on ethnic marriage. No status difference exists for any of the categories except for the older generation Catholics from rural areas (notably, the German Catholics). Size of hometown has more influence on the older generations than it does on the newer arrivals, who are still more ethnically cohesive.

It is generation—the length of family residence in this country—that has the most consistent and important influence on ethnic intermarriage. The newer generations are not distinguished by hometown or class background. It is among the older generations of Catholic Americans where marital assimilation shows variation. The variation itself is clear with the ethnic persistence of the Germans of rural America and to some degree the endogamy of the Polish Catholics in the cities.

THE INFLUENCE OF EDUCATION

Prominent among the alternative notions of assimilation which have been fashionable in the intellectual and social history of the United States is that complex of ideas called Anglo-American conformity, or as it was also called at the height of its popularity in the first third of this century, the Americanization movement (Gordon, 1964, pp. 88–114). This point of view emphasized the visible acculturation of American ethnic groups, all of whom were to adopt the cultural values and norms of the host society of Anglo-Americans. Americanization, it was argued, would take place most rapidly and efficiently with developing widespread education (Higham, 1963, pp. 234–263).

Although not explicit to the body of the notion, as it is in the idea of the melting pot, intermarriage is implicit in Americanization. Exogamy would follow the acculturation of immigrant groups, since it was expected that Americanization would lead to less visible differentiation among white foreign-born groups and their descendents and would promote greater integration and social unity. The early proponents of this movement relied chiefly on the schools to further "ethnic unity" among the culturally diverse (Higham, 1963, p. 235). An educator in New York went so far as to predict in 1902 that "education will solve every problem of our national life, even that of assimilating our foreign element" (Buchanan, 1902, p. 691; quoted in Higham, 1963).

Table 23.   Type of Ethnic Marriage by Level of Education, and Per Cent Exogamous by Ethnicity and Level of Education

Type of Ethnic Marriage	Level of Education					
	6th Grade or Less	7th or 8th Grade	Some High School	All High School	Some College	College Graduate or More
Endogamy	87	66	58	47	47	38
Exogamy	13	34	42	53	53	62
Total	100	100	100	100	100	100
	(71)	(184)	(253)	(380)	(131)	(77)

Ethnicity	Level of Education	
	Some High School and Less	High School Graduate and More
Irish	63	55
	(38)	(142)
Eastern European	58	56
	(62)	(66)
German	47	62
	(62)	(103)
Polish	42	57
	(69)	(63)
French-Canadian	22	46
	(64)	(48)
Italian	21	47
	(130)	(126)
Spanish-speaking	10	18
	(70)	(17)
Total	35	54
	(508)	(588)

$$N = 1,096$$
$$\text{NA education} = 1$$
$$\text{Total} = 1,097$$

Education then would challenge the traditional endogamous values of the ethnic culture, as well as increase the opportunities to meet and marry someone from a different ethnic background. The extent to which educational level does influence the type of ethnic marriage contracted by contemporary Catholics is presented in Table 23.

The relationship is strong and positive; ethnic exogamy increases with level of education. For Catholic Americans with a sixth-grade education or less, only 13 per cent are exogamous. The proportion of the intermarried increases to a high of 62 per cent of those Catholics who have completed a college education or more. It is worth pointing out that the influence of only some years of college (as opposed to having a college degree) is no greater than being a high school graduate. It is being a graduate of four years or more of higher education that makes a bigger difference in the choice of ethnic spouse.

The early proponents of the Americanization thesis were quite correct in understanding the force of education for assimilating the immigrants. As Table 23 also indicates, the level of education is particularly meaningful for the Italians (47 per cent of the better educated intermarried, as opposed to only 21 per cent of the lesser educated) and the French-Canadians (46 in contrast to 22 per cent). The Polish and German Catholics show important but less intense differences.

Aside from the fact that the Spanish-speaking Puerto Ricans and Mexicans and the combined Eastern European group are not as influenced by the level of education, an important and unique fact of Table 23 refers to the Irish. Among Irish Catholics, it is the *lesser* educated who are more likely to become exogamous. In fact, the Irish with some secondary schooling or less are the most exogamous of all ethnic groups in this category.

This Irish reversal suggests an interesting phenomenon. As presented in Chapter Two, the Irish are the highest among all Catholic groups in the completion of high school and the attainment of a college education. The finding just presented here indicates that there may be a distinction in the type of schooling between the better educated and the lesser educated Irish, a distinction that could account for the greater exogamy among the less educated group.

The better educated Irish may have attended parochial schools with a preponderance of fellow Irish schoolmates, and this could explain the tendency toward in-group marriage. The less educated Irish may have attended public schools with their greater ethnic and religious heterogeneity, thereby facilitating exogamy. The data of the survey used here do not include the ethnic composition of schools attended, but they do emphasize the factor of Catholic parochial schooling. Catholic schools are often disproportionately ethnic, especially in regions where certain nationality backgrounds predominate among Catholics. This is true not only because of residential patterns in the environment of the schools and the nature of the nationality parishes, but also because of the greater inclination of some ethnic groups to support them (Rossi and Rossi, 1961; Greeley and Rossi, 1966).

Table 24. Per Cent Who Are High School Graduates or More, by Ethnicity and Type of Schooling

Ethnicity	Type of Schooling	
	Only Public Schooling	All or Some Catholic Schooling
Irish	55	86
	(38)	(141)
Eastern European	54	49
	(54)	(72)
German	53	67
	(58)	(107)
Italian	51	46
	(176)	(80)
Polish	44	48
	(32)	(102)
French-Canadian	37	43
	(19)	(92)
Spanish-speaking	20	22
	(69)	(18)
Total	47	59
	(456)	(636)

$$N = 1,092$$
$$\text{NA education} = \quad 1$$
$$\text{NA schooling} = \quad 4$$
$$\text{Total} = 1,097$$

The assumption about the Irish differential between types of schools and the level of education is confirmed quite strongly by the data of Table 24. For the total sample of Catholics, there is the fact that Catholics who went to parochial schools are more likely to have attained a higher level of education (Greeley and Rossi, 1966). For the Irish, however, the magnitude of the difference is 31 percentage points; as many as 86 per cent of the Irish with Catholic schooling completed high school requirements and went further, whereas only 55 per cent of the public school Irish did the same. For no other ethnic group is the difference so pronounced. Clearly, then, among the different ethnic styles of Catholic life in the United States, the merger of educational success and parochial school involvement is a distinctly Irish phenomenon.

To determine the extent of support given the parochial school system by other ethnic groups, consider the raw data of Table 24 where the number of respondents with parochial or public schooling (given in the parentheses) indicates the variability of such support. More will be said about this specifically in Chapter Five, but reassembled data of the same factors can reverse the direction of the percentages and provide a view of this variability, with a control for level of education instead of kind of schooling (Abramson, 1969, p. 111).

The Irish association between higher education and Catholic schooling is strong enough to read the same way with the percentage direction change; only 54 per cent of the Irish dropouts had some Catholic schooling, in contrast to 85 per cent of the Irish high school graduates. The Germans show a much slighter suggestion of this phenomenon, but for all other groups there are no differences. The French-Canadians, regardless of the level of education, had over 80 per cent of their children attending the parochial schools, and the Polish Catholics are next highest in involvement with 75 per cent of both their high school dropouts and graduates with parochial schooling. The two groups with the least support for the Catholic school system are the Italians and the Spanish-speaking Mexicans and Puerto Ricans. Less than one-third of these groups, regardless of dropping out of high school or graduating, had any formal Catholic education.

It is reasonable, in view of these findings, to expect the type of school attended to have an effect on ethnic marriage. The fact that younger Irish and French-Canadian Catholics were shown in Table 20 to be more exogamous than the older members of their ethnic groups is no doubt a function of parochial school involvement. Table 25 offers the percentage of those with a high school education who attend Catholic high schools, with the control for age.

For the total figures in Table 25, there is general evidence of increased attendance in Catholic high schools among younger Catholics in their twenties and thirties. The pattern obtains for every group shown, but the greater differences emerge for the Irish and French-Canadians. A clear majority of the younger Irish and French-Canadians received their high school education in the Catholic system, as opposed to one-third or less of the older respondents from these two groups. The influence of the religioethnic school would indeed weaken the influence of age, with regard to ethnic marriage.

A direct examination of the effect that the type of school has on marriage begins in Table 26, which presents the percentage exogamous by types of elementary school and high school. Consider in the first two columns the type of elementary school. The total figures show no difference, but these mask the influences shown for specific ethnicities. Both the Irish and the French-Canadians reveal greater exogamy among their public school mem-

Table 25.   Per Cent Attending Catholic High Schools, by Ethnicity and Age

Ethnicity	Age of Respondent	
	Twenties to Thirties	Forties to Fifties
Irish	57	34
	(97)	(70)
French-Canadian	53	21
	(47)	(28)
German	42	30
	(67)	(60)
Polish	33	21
	(46)	(52)
Eastern European	25	16
	(40)	(56)
Italian	14	6
	(104)	(101)
Spanish-speaking	6	0
	(32)	(6)[a]
Total	35	20
	(451)	(385)

$$N = 836$$
No high school = 255
NA high school = 2
NA age = 4
$$\text{Total} - 1,097$$

[a] Too few cases for adequate percentaging.

bers. Those Irish and especially the French-Canadians with elementary education in the Catholic school system tend to be more endogamous in their respective groups. Because of the high support these two nationalities give the parochial school institutions, it seems safe to assume that the Catholic schools which they do attend are ethnically Irish or French-Canadian.

One might expect, on the other hand, that ethnic groups with typically low support of the Catholic school system (as measured by less involvement) would show greater ethnic exogamy when they do attend such schools. Of the Italians and Spanish-speaking, for example, who have attended parochial schools, one might look for signs of ethnic exogamy because they would be mingling with predominantly non-Italian and non-Spanish-speaking Catholic students. Furthermore, for public school educated Italians, Mexicans, and

Table 26.   Per Cent Exogamous, by Ethnicity and Type of Schooling

Ethnicity	Type of Elementary School		Type of High School	
	All or Some Catholic	Only Public	All or Some Catholic	Only Public
German	55	59	61	63
	(102)	(63)	(46)	(81)
Eastern European	54	64	58	62
	(69)	(58)	(19)	(78)
Irish	54	65	51	62
	(139)	(40)	(80)	(89)
Polish	50	52	50	53
	(102)	(33)	(26)	(72)
Italian	32	34	52	35
	(78)	(178)	(21)	(184)
French-Canadian	27	52	29	43
	(91)	(21)	(31)	(44)
Spanish-speaking	22	9	67	22
	(18)	(69)	(3)[a]	(36)
Total	47	43	53	50
	(621)	(474)	(237)	(603)

$N = 1,095$ $N = 840$

NA schooling = 2   No high school = 255

NA schooling = 2

Total = 1,097   Total = 1,097

[a] Too few cases for adequate percentaging.

Puerto Ricans, one might anticipate the suggestion of group endogamy; because they prefer to attend the public schools, and because of residential ethnic enclaves in and around the elementary school districts, there is the greater chance for Italians and the Spanish-speaking to meet others in their respective groups in the public system.

Table 26 shows no difference for the Italians. It appears that Catholic elementary schools have no effect on Italian marriage patterns. For the Puerto Ricans and Mexicans, however, the parochial schools had considerable influence; only 9 per cent of the Spanish-speaking from the public schools intermarried with other ethnic groups, but as many as 22 per cent of those from the parochial system did.

It would be more direct to consider this association at the high school level, since these years of education are closer to the time of marriage. The second two columns of Table 26 provide these data, and the same findings persist. The total figures disguise the ethnic components. The Irish and the French-Canadians with parochial school backgrounds are less likely to marry out of their groups. The Italians, at this level of education, do show the expected pattern; only one-third of the public school educated Italians are exogamous, but more than half of the parochial school Italians are. The Spanish-speaking also display the expected result, but the thin case load of parochial school educated Mexicans and Puerto Ricans is inadequate for any confirmation.

In all of these data on type of school background, the Polish and German Catholics show no difference in the proportions of their members becoming exogamous. In contrast to the Irish and the French-Canadians who show signs of exogamy with public school education, and the Italians and Spanish-speaking who reflect the reverse behavior, the marriage patterns of the Poles and Germans remain constant.

This might be explained by the presumed ethnic composition of schools attended, data for which are presently unavailable. Public and parochial schools in the vicinity of Polish and German neighborhoods may simply reflect ethnic mixture, and the probability of Polish and German students meeting Catholics of other nationality backgrounds is the same in both types of school systems. Parochial schools attended by Polish and German Catholics may not be quite as homogeneous, then, as those attended by Irish and French-Canadian Catholics.

This is better understood in the light of regional concentrations. The Irish and the French-Canadians predominate, as Chapter Two pointed out, in the heavily Catholic regions of New England and the East. As the most involved in the Catholic school system to begin with, their parochial schools are also likely to find a majority of students being Irish and French-Canadians.

In regions where the Poles are numerous (such as the East North Central) and where the Germans are concentrated (West North Central), the situation is, as Joseph Fichter (1964) has described it, more of ethnic mingling in the parochial school system itself. This is due not only to the relative lack of Catholics in the total population (thus producing fewer parochial schools), but also to the somewhat less intense involvement of the Polish and German Catholics in the religious system, and the greater spread of ethnic backgrounds in the Middle West.

One can conclude, with reference to the "Americanization" thesis of education and assimilation, that within the realm of American Catholicism at least, increased education does indeed lead to more ethnic exogamy, with the qualifications discussed. The issue of the type of school, however, becomes crucial for the specific ethnic groups involved.

ETHNICITY AS A RELIGIOCULTURAL FORCE

One of the intervening questions in the study of parochial school attendance, as Andrew Greeley and Peter Rossi (1966) analyze it, is the associated level of parental religious involvement in the home. It has been demonstrated that those who are most likely to go to parochial schools are those from more religious homes, homes where the externals of religious duty are fairly well observed. Any presumed effect of parochial school education may, in fact, be due to the predisposition of parental religious influence. Thus ethnic endogamy or exogamy may be a function of the level of parental religiousness rather than ethnic involvement in public or parochial schooling. This problem would not require the clarification it does if the exogamy under question were religious, that is, intermarriage between Catholics and non-Catholics. But the form of exogamy is ethnic, and intra-Catholic, and as such, levels of parental religiousness will connote other considerations of a peculiarly ethnic nature.

What are the differences, say, between highly religious Irish Catholic homes and less religious Irish Catholic homes? This becomes the essential question. One might assume that the difference is not only religious (i.e., differentials in Mass attendance, or in parochial school involvement) but also ethnic (i.e., different levels of ethnic exogamy).

Because of historical associations often involving the interrelationship of nationality and religion, about which more will be said in the following two chapters, I am arguing that for those ethnic groups for whom religion and ethnicity are traditionally interwoven there will be changes of an ethnic nature following from religious differences, as well as religious changes following from ethnic differences.

The answer to the first part of this problem, that of ethnic changes following from religious differences, is necessarily confined in this book to the extent of ethnic exogamy. The possible relevance of other ethnic considerations, such as changes in language use, the extent of community, and the question of identification, can also be empirically examined and should be worthwhile questions for future research in the sociology of ethnicity and religion.

For changes in ethnic marriage, the data of Table 27 offer the percentage exogamous by the level of parental religiousness.[3] All parents are Catholic, and levels of religiousness are limited to the degree of observation of formal requirements. The levels are derived from an index with four categories (Greeley and Rossi, 1966, p. 44): a measure of 3 is highest (both parents are weekly Mass-goers, and at least one receives Communion weekly); a measure of 2 (both parents are weekly Mass-goers, but neither receives weekly Communion); a measure of 1 (at least one parent attends Mass once a

Table 27.   Per Cent Exogamous, by Ethnicity and Religious Background

Ethnicity	Religious Background	
	High Parental Religiousness	Low Parental Religiousness
German	53 (122)	67 (36)
Irish	52 (130)	66 (44)
Eastern European	51 (76)	66 (50)
Polish	48 (90)	56 (41)
Italian	35 (95)	32 (158)
French-Canadian	28 (79)	48 (23)
Spanish-speaking	8 (25)	13 (60)
Total	45 (653)	45 (440)

$$N = 1,093$$
$$\text{NA religiousness} = 4$$
$$\text{Total} = 1,097$$

week); and a measure of 0 (all other Catholic parents). Table 27 divides parental religiousness into high level (measures of 3 and 2) and low level (measures of 1 and 0).

It appears from Table 27 that whereas the total figures show absolutely no difference by level of parental religiousness and the percentage differences for the Italian and Spanish-speaking Catholics are negligible, the other five groups show varying increases in exogamy with low religious background. The largest difference is for the French-Canadians; only 28 per cent of those from highly religious homes married out of the group, whereas almost half of the French-Canadians from less religious backgrounds did so. The fact that the Italians, Mexicans, and Puerto Ricans all show no comparable difference may attest to the noted indifference of these nationality groups to their formal religious system. More will be said of this subsequently.

In general, Table 27 suggests the phenomenon of a religioethnic force, where the Church means some degree of Irishness to the Irish Catholics, something of Quebec culture to the French-Canadians, and so forth. It is important to keep in mind that all marriages are with other Roman Catholics, whether ethnically endogamous or exogamous. The changes are within the Church.

Table 28 follows up this direction of analysis with a control for type of school attended. For the Irish, the pattern persists, especially among those educated in the public schools. Catholic schooling counters the influence of low parental religiousness among the Irish, just as parental religiousness weakens the influence of the public school.

For the French-Canadians, there is a steady progression of ethnic assimilation, with proportions of exogamy increasing from a low of 27 per cent among those from more religious homes and educated in parochial schools, to a high of 56 per cent among the public schooled Franco-Americans from less

Table 28.   Per Cent Exogamous, by Ethnicity, Type of Schooling, and Religious Background

Ethnicity	Catholic Schooling		Public Schooling	
	High Religious	Low Religious	High Religious	Low Religious
German	53	63	51	74
	(88)	(19)	(39)	(19)
Irish	52	61	54	83
	(107)	(33)	(26)	(12)
Eastern European	49	65	59	68
	(45)	(26)	(29)	(25)
Polish	49	52	44	63
	(78)	(25)	(16)	(16)
Italian	40	27	32	35
	(35)	(45)	(60)	(116)
French-Canadian	27	35	50	56
	(75)	(17)	(10)	(9)[a]
Spanish-speaking	14	27	6	10
	(7)[a]	(11)	(18)	(49)
Total	47	49	42	43
	(450)	(185)	(203)	(251)

$$N = 1,089$$
$$\text{NA religiousness} = 4$$
$$\text{NA schooling} = 4$$

$$\text{Total} = 1,097$$

[a] Too few cases for adequate percentaging.

religious homes. The influence of parochial schooling and religious background maintains the traditional French-Canadian ethnic community in the United States. The larger influence is the type of school, but the two factors are additive in their effect on French-Canadians.

For the Germans, Poles, and Eastern Europeans in Table 28, parental religiousness seems to be more influential than type of school attended, as expected from previous discussions. For the Italians, the only appreciable difference is among those with a Catholic education, and the influence runs in the reverse. Italians from *more* religious backgrounds, in the category of parochial schooling, are the ones more likely to become exogamous. The combination of Catholic schooling and higher parental religiousness does facilitate Italian intermarriage. Since both of these factors have traditionally been unexceptional in the Italian subculture, the fact of their presence (although characterizing only a minority of Italian Catholics) and the fact of their correlation with intermarriage help to signify the changes in the religioethnic composition of Italian American Catholicism. It is in a sense only this minority of Italians who are said to be becoming "Irish" in terms of mobility within the Church and within the larger society (Herberg, 1955; Glazer and Moynihan, 1963, 1970; Russo, 1968, 1970).

Finally, an argument can be offered with regard to the factor of generation. The association between exogamy and the older generations is so strong (excepting the German Catholics) that it might well eliminate any influence of parental religiousness. Among the older generation Catholics, the level of religiousness in the home ought not make any appreciable difference. The drift toward exogamy, it is expected, will prevail regardless of the degree of religious observance. And too, presumably, the older generations are that much further removed from the constraints and religioethnic intensity of the traditional Church.

Table 29 examines this question and shows the persistence of the Irish and the French-Canadian patterns. For these two groups, the percentage exogamous continues to be higher among the less religious backgrounds, for both generations. The differences in both cases are smaller for the older generations, which indicates the influence of cultural change, but the expression of generational continuity is clear.

The German Catholics offer no difference, as expected, for the older generations. Furthermore, the proclivity of the newer generation Germans to intermarry is even stronger among those from less religious backgrounds; as many as three out of four of the new generation Germans from less religious homes intermarry and move away from the German group. Religious background does not appear to influence the Italians of either generation, or the Poles of the first and second generation.

Table 29. Per Cent Exogamous, by Ethnicity, Generation in the United States, and Religious Background

Ethnicity	Newer Generation		Older Generation	
	High Religious	Low Religious	High Religious	Low Religious
German	58	76	51	53
	(38)	(21)	(84)	(15)
Eastern European	48	64	67	100
	(61)	(47)	(15)	(3)[a]
Polish	45	50	56	69
	(65)	(28)	(25)	(13)
Irish	42	60	58	68
	(45)	(10)	(85)	(34)
Italian	29	28	59	57
	(78)	(137)	(17)	(21)
French-Canadian	17	36	48	58
	(52)	(11)	(27)	(12)
Spanish-speaking	8	13	0	14
	(24)	(53)	(1)[a]	(7)[a]
Total	37	39	56	61
	(368)	(312)	(266)	(114)

$$N = 1,060$$
DK generation = 31
NA generation = 1
NA religiousness = 5

Total = 1,097

[a] Too few cases for adequate percentaging.

SUMMARY

The thrust of this chapter has been an investigation of some of the important factors, all antecedent in time, which influence the type of marriage for Catholic ethnic groups. The major societal predictors of ethnic exogamy are generation in the United States (longer residence), size of hometown (urban settlements), and level of education (higher attainments). Endogamy and the traditional ethnic community, on the other hand, are maintained by more recent American residence, rural and small-town life, and lower associations in formal education.

The latter factor of education is essentially qualified into public and parochial school systems. The influence of Catholic education itself suggests the relevance of the level of parental religiousness in the home of origin, and this points to the religioethnic background of the different Catholic groups as essentially relevant to the study of ethnic change.[4]

Societal and religious factors were discussed in their general correlation with type of marriage, but the ethnic factor produced certain important exceptions and discoveries. The facts that the more likely candidates for ethnic intermarriage are the more recent German immigrants (rather than the older generation Germans), the rural Polish Catholics (as opposed to the urban Polish Catholics), and the less educated Irish (in contrast to the more educated Irish), all signify unique ethnic characteristics and processes. The deviance of these groups to the norms at work in the larger society and religious system not only helps to emphasize the patterns noted and discussed but also underlines the importance of the idea of ethnic variability and diversity in America's past and present.

The discussion of ethnic variation within the religious confines of the American Catholic Church leads to a specific investigation of cultural heterogeneity and diverse religioethnic styles. The following two chapters examine directly the diversity of religiousness and compares the traditional orientations of Catholic ethnic groups toward their shared religion.

NOTES

1. The data on Catholic populations are gathered from different diocesan sources and are neither standardized nor always accurate. Their use here is for their approximation to the best available estimates. States included in these U.S. Census-designated regions are listed in note 2 of Chapter Two.

2. The Duncan scale runs from a low rating of 1 to a high rating of 10. For a description of this scale, see Duncan (1961).

3. The second part of this problem, that of religious changes following from ethnic differences, is the subject of Chapter Seven.

4. One major analytical difficulty of this chapter is the step-by-step procedure of the examination of causal sequence. It should be clear that the influence of antecedent variables on exogamy would be better understood if controls could have been made simultaneously. Due to the size problem of cases in this sample, it was not possible. Reservations, therefore, need

to be raised for the presumed order of influence of the variables examined.

Part Three

Religious Diversity among Catholics

CHAPTER FIVE

TRADITIONAL RELIGIOETHNIC INVOLVEMENT

Coming from parts of Europe historically distant and separate from each other, from the western coast of Ireland to the eastern slopes of the Carpathians, the newcomers brought with them different and decided notions as to what was the proper form of the Church, wished each to perpetuate the unique qualities of the religious life they had practiced at home.

OSCAR HANDLIN (1951)

...the Church is not only essentially transcendent; it is also, through its members, incarnate in a given time and place. Through its members, it affects a culture and is affected, for better or worse, by the local conditions and challenges that its members meet. In this sense, it assumes that "garb" of which Gibbons spoke. In this sense, we can distinguish "Catholicism" in France, in Ireland, in Italy—or in America. Distinguishing, we can see that differences in attitude and behavior, sometimes minor, sometimes important, exist in the Catholic climate in various times and places.

WILLIAM P. CLANCY (1953)

SOCIOLOGISTS OF RELIGION have glossed over the meaning of heterogeneity within American Catholicism and have ignored the challenge to study the variations of ethnic traditions within the common religion. To be sure, historians (Barry, 1953; Cross, 1958) have examined the political and ideological struggles of the structure of the Church—struggles which reflect underlying diversity—and sociologists have often described the institutional nature of the different nationality parishes (Park and Miller, 1921; Nuesse and Harte, 1951). But the implications of past and present diversity for socioreligious behavior have been left relatively untouched.

Recent essays and empirical studies of the role of religion in American society, following the route of the triple melting pot, have structured the fact of religion in terms of broad socioreligious categories. Will Herberg (1955) and Gerhard Lenski (1961), two prominent writers on the sociology of religion, assume a contemporary homogeneous Protestant, Catholic, and Jewish population, limited only by race. Herberg, more than Lenski, acknowledges the historical ethnic heterogeneity of the Catholic Church in America, but both assume the irrelevance of the ethnic factor for contemporary social behavior. This needs to be tested, directly and comparatively.

The historical association of ethnic nationality and religion (which is background to the concerns in Chapter Six) is clearly documented, but the legacy of the ethnic church in American society is not well understood. The theologian H. Richard Niebuhr (1957, pp. 106–107) has pointed out, more clearly than many, the influence of cultural, social, and regional forces on religious differentiation:

> Among the social forces which contribute to the formation of classes and so to the schism of churches, economic factors may be the most powerful; but they are not the only sources of denominationalism. Sometimes, indeed, they seem to be less important than ethnic and political or generally cultural factors. . . . A realistic analysis of the American religious scene shows that its variegated pattern has been drawn to a large extent by European immigrants who have made the United States the crucible of many churches as well as the melting-pot of many races.

Niebuhr applied this thesis to a study of Protestant denominations, but as J. Milton Yinger (1963, pp. 100–101) has suggested, the idea of ethnic or cultural diversity refers to Catholicism (and other religions) as well:

Denominations, to be sure, do not appear within the structure of Catholicism, but the great diversity of the membership of the Catholic Church is reflected in the wide range of its activities and styles of communication . . . .Those who picture it as a monolithic structure, homogeneous in outlook and uniform in influence, fail to recognize the degree to which religion is affected by culture, class, occupation, educational level, and other secular facts.

One of the purposes of this section is to look into the meaning of the ethnically plural Church, and to examine this religion in terms of its cultural diversity rather than its homogeneity. The literature on immigration and the adjustment of immigrant groups to American life is filled with reports of the various contributions of nationality groups to the United States and their respective religions.[1] To one familiar with this history, the Irish are foremost in the institutionalization of the Catholic Church in America (Potter, 1960; Shannon, 1963). Obvious explanations for organizational success among the Irish in the field of religion usually refer to their facility with the English language and their relatively early arrival in the mid-nineteenth century.

The question of traditional religioethnic involvement within Catholicism, however, remains to be examined comparatively. How do the other major ethnic groups compare with the Irish in terms of associational involvement within the Church? To what degree does the level of social class and generation in America make any difference in religioethnic behavior? From the historical point of view, what kinds of backgrounds and cultural orientations did the Catholic immigrant groups bring with them to the United States, and how might these be said to relate to one another, with respect to a common Catholicity? After determining something about religioethnic involvement, to what extent can one talk of a sociologically homogeneous Church today, following an American and European experience of social, religious, and ethnic diversity?

These are the questions that guide this section of the book. Catholicity, as used here, is defined as religious or church involvement within associational Catholicism. The emphasis on behavioral involvement, as opposed to more attitudinal dimensions, is crucial. It is important to distinguish this meaning from any overtones of "religiosity" because the discussion will not suggest any differences in underlying feelings or belief systems, or in any aspects of subjective piety and personal devotion.[2]

The emphasis on involvement lies in affiliation and attachment to *formal* Church commitments. It suggests the degree to which an individual Catholic associates with his religion by following explicit requirements. In a sense, the subject of inquiry here is the visible religion. The scope of this book does not warrant the assumption that behavioral indicators of religious involvement lead to necessarily similar directions for attitudes (Greeley and Rossi, 1966).

Another important consideration is the nominal universality of the formal requirements in Roman Catholicism. Theologically, the Church is very much concerned with associational involvement, through liturgical requirements of weekly attendance at Mass and other defined standards. These are clearly expressed requirements, especially in contrast to the less formalized expectations of Judaism and Protestantism, and as such, they exercise a modal influence over all Catholics, regardless of nationality (Fichter, 1954). Thus the very universality of formal religious requirements serves as a standard against which variations by nationality or culture may be examined.

This chapter will document the extent of ethnic diversity among Catholic Americans in terms of religious associational involvement. Comparison is made of the seven largest ethnic categories: the Irish, Italians, Germans, Poles, French-Canadians, Spanish-speaking Puerto Ricans and Mexicans, and Eastern Europeans (the latter including here the Lithuanians). Religioethnic behavior is controlled also by the generation and class background of the ethnic groups.

Following the analysis of religious behavior for these groups, I shall examine the historical development of Catholicity for six American ethnic groups, to clarify the roots of diversity. In the process, I will explore a few of the major patterns in the comparative relationship of religion and nationality.

ETHNIC DIVERSITY

The data in this section refer mainly to the ethnically endogamous parents of the respondents of the survey. Chapter Seven will relate the extent of diversity for the respondents themselves, both endogamous and exogamous, but the major concern of the present discussion is the traditional distinctions of religioethnic behavior, for which the endogamous parental generation is presumably the more appropriate population.[3]

Table 30 shows the extent of involvement as reported for the parents of the respondents. To begin, consider the first two columns of the table. For fathers as well as mothers, three ethnic groups are the most involved in attendance at Mass: the Irish, the French-Canadians, and the Germans. Somewhat less intensely involved are the Poles and the Eastern Europeans, both of whom tend to level at the "average" reported for all ethnically endogamous parents. Distinctly least associated with going to weekly church services are the Italian and Spanish-speaking Catholics.[4]

A point might be made of the sex differences between mothers and fathers in church attendance. For every ethnic group, women are more likely

Table 30. Parental Religious Behavior by Ethnicity (Per Cent at Weekly Mass Attendance, Monthly Communion, and Support of Parochial Schooling)

Ethnicity	Weekly Mass Attendance		Monthly Communion		Some or All Catholic Elementary Schooling	Some or All Catholic High School
	Mother	Father	Mother	Father		
Irish	91 (163)	81 (160)	79 (150)	62 (142)	87 (135)	62 (122)
French-Canadian	89 (115)	80 (115)	80 (103)	61 (99)	88 (100)	67 (55)
German	89 (170)	82 (169)	74 (163)	60 (159)	81 (106)	54 (59)
Polish	81 (147)	76 (148)	62 (133)	40 (127)	87 (120)	31 (81)
Eastern European	76 (140)	66 (138)	52 (124)	31 (114)	68 (93)	37 (59)
Italian	71 (300)	39 (294)	61 (266)	23 (249)	35 (215)	14 (149)
Spanish-speaking	58 (108)	36 (107)	55 (78)	24 (74)	35 (65)	9 (32)
Total	79 (1,162)	63 (1,148)	66 (1,033)	42 (980)	67 (850)	39 (573)

	Weekly Mass Attendance		Monthly Communion		Elementary	High School
	N = 1,162	N = 1,148	N = 1,033	N = 980	N = 850	N = 573
	DK = 28	DK = 42	DK = 156	DK = 208	None available = 339	None available = 329
	NA = 4	NA = 4	NA = 5	NA = 6	No schooling = 2	No schooling = 289
					NA schooling = 3	NA schooling = 3
	Total = 1,194[a]	= 1,194[a]	= 1,194[a]	= 1,194[a]	= 1,194[a]	= 1,194[a]

[a] The total N of 1,194 represents the working case total for most tables in this chapter. It is the sum of all ethnically endogamous parental couples with both spouses Catholic. Excluded are 298 ethnically exogamous parents, 496 non-Catholic parents, and 83 parents with nonapplicable ethnicity.

than men to go to Mass. Not unexpectedly, this fact is consistent with previous research on the sex difference in religious association, for both the United States and Europe (Fichter, 1952; Fogarty, 1957; Demerath, 1965; Greeley and Rossi, 1966).

A comparison of the sex difference in Table 30 suggests something else as well. The differences between the sexes are considerably greater for the less involved ethnic groups. It might appear that the more highly involved endogamous groups absorb some of the underlying sex differential in religious practice, whereas the less involved Italians and Spanish-speaking may be emphasizing the traditional stances of males and females in going to church.[5]

The diversity shown for attendance at Mass is strengthened by the data on frequency with which parents are reported as having received Communion. The middle two columns of Table 30 offer these percentages, and the rank orders for mothers and fathers are again roughly the same here as they were for Mass attendance. The Irish, the French-Canadians, and the Germans are the groups most frequently receiving Communion, and again the differences are considerably greater between the Italian and Spanish-speaking parents than they are for the five other groups shown.

In addition to the measures of Mass attendance and Communion reception, diversity among Catholics is manifest in the degree of traditional support offered the parochial school system of the Church. The last two columns of Table 30 present the proportions of each group of ethnic parents who provided their children (the respondents of the survey) with at least some years of Catholic education at the elementary and high school levels. Those Catholics for whom parochial schools were not available are excluded from the analysis.

The French-Canadian involvement in the Catholic school system is the highest, at both levels of education. Almost nine out of ten French-Canadian homes sent their children to Catholic elementary schools, and two-thirds of these homes supported the parochial high schools as well. The Irish attendance at the Catholic schools is virtually as high, and the remaining five groups show diminishing support. An important exception to the anticipated pattern is the very high Polish involvement in the Catholic school system at the elementary level; at the high school level, the Polish support is intermediate in position again, between the higher and lower proportions.

In general, the rank orders of associational involvement in Catholicism are closely aligned for the different ethnic groups. The Irish, the French-Canadians, and the Germans (somewhat less than the first two groups) are the most frequently involved in the formal religious and educational requirements of the Church. The Poles and Eastern Europeans, although relatively high in their association, do not emerge with the same consistent intensity of involvement that characterizes the first three groups. The Italians, the Mexicans, and the Puerto Ricans all display the least amount of association;

theirs is a patterned indifference to the formalized religious and educational role of Church life.

THE GENERATION FACTOR: HERBERG AND LENSKI REVISITED

Differences of religious association among Catholic ethnic groups in the United States may not be caused by the factor of ethnicity as directly as Table 30 would have us believe. It might easily be argued, and often is, that these presumably ethnic relationships are merely reflections of the influence of generation in America. Will Herberg (1955) and Gerhard Lenski (1961), among others, have called attention to the idea that increased "Americanization" (as measured, for example, by generational background) leads to more church attendance and participation in voluntary associations. Since the most involved nationalities—all of Western European origin—are those that include a good share of the earlier immigrants to the United States, their higher religious involvement might be due to the fact of their having more established roots in the American society.

The Herberg hypothesis in particular explains that the increase in church attendance (and presumably religious identification as well) takes the form of a religious resurgence after an experience of religious decline. Basing his argument on Marcus Hansen's (1938, 1952) "principle of third-generation interest," Herberg articulates the idea that the first-generation immigrants bring to America the ethnic form of religion traditional to their country of origin and seek to perpetuate its form in the adopted society. The second generation, the children of the immigrants, come to reject some aspects of their ancestral culture in their desire to become "more Americanized" and thus lose interest in the ethnic form of their parental religion.

The emergence of the third generation, the grandchildren of the immigrants, means an alteration in this process. Having become culturally assimilated to American values and norms, the third generation also develops an appreciation of the place religion has in the larger American society. At the same time, the third generation becomes interested in the religion of the grandparents, in spite of (or because of) the fact that the church and the religion are not exactly in the same form they were when transplanted by the immigrants. Thus Herberg explains increased religiousness among the third generation, after some decline among the second generation. Given only in broad outline here, the Herberg hypothesis is provocative and has received a good deal of attention.

Lenski's empirical test of this idea puts forth a modification. Lenski found, among Catholics of his survey in Detroit, that instead of a decline and return there was evidence of a steady progression of increasing church attendance with generational residence in America. Neither Lenski in his empirical analysis, nor Herberg in his expository essay, considers the ethnic factor as a contemporary variable within associational religion.

What kind of support for the Herberg or Lenski position does the control for ethnic background in these data offer? To what extent is the ethnic differential in Mass attendance among Catholic Americans due to generational experience in the United States? Table 31 provides some answers to

Table 31. Parental Church Attendance by Ethnicity and Generation (Per Cent at Weekly Mass Attendance)

| Ethnicity | Generation in the United States | | | | | |
| | Mother | | | Father | | |
	First	Second	Third	First	Second	Third
Irish	96	87	91	86	81	77
	(47)	(38)	(75)	(51)	(31)	(74)
French-Canadian	95	100	70	89	91	59
	(62)	(19)	(27)	(57)	(22)	(29)
German	82	87	94	69	88	90
	(56)	(39)	(68)	(62)	(32)	(68)
Polish	78	85	77	74	86	54
	(83)	(46)	(13)	(94)	(35)	(13)
Eastern European	73	92	67	62	83	83
	(107)	(26)	(6)[a]	(114)	(18)	(6)[a]
Italian	72	68	78	40	34	38
	(224)	(66)	(9)[a]	(253)	(32)	(8)[a]
Spanish-speaking	59	58	50	38	33	20
	(85)	(12)	(10)	(92)	(3)[a]	(10)
Total	76	81	85	58	74	72
	(669)	(249)	(219)	(727)	(177)	(218)

$$N = 1,137 \qquad\qquad = 1,122$$
$$\text{DK generation} = 26 \qquad = 26$$
$$\text{NA generation} = 2 \qquad = 2$$
$$\text{DK attendance} = 25 \qquad = 40$$
$$\text{NA attendance} = 4 \qquad = 4$$

$$\text{Total} = 1,194 \qquad = 1,194$$

[a] Too few cases for adequate percentaging.

these questions, with the data for the ethnically endogamous parental generation of this survey.

Fathers and mothers of the first generation are those who were born abroad, and these constitute the majority of the respondents' parents. Second-generation parents are those born in the United States, with the respondent's grandparents born abroad. And third- or later-generation parents refer to those born in the United States, with one to four of the respondent's grandparents also born in this country.

It is apparent in the data of Table 31 that generational background does not eliminate the ethnic factor in religious behavior. Indeed, it strengthens it. The first-generation Irish and French-Canadians are by far the most involved of all Catholic groups shown, and this is true for the church attendance of both sexes. The Germans, the Poles, and the Eastern Europeans, of the first generation, are at intermediate levels of church association, and the immigrant Italians, Mexicans, and Puerto Ricans are still among the least involved.

Furthermore, there are as a result of holding generational background constant curious indications of religious change. Consider first the total figures for all Catholic fathers and mothers. These serve as a gross confirmation of the Lenski findings and a rejection of the Herberg hypothesis. Without the control for ethnicity, there is the pattern of increased church-going as generation in the United States increases. There is no suggestion of any decline among the second generation.

Consider also the variability of this pattern for the different ethnic groups. For the German, Polish, and Eastern European Catholics, there is clearly a pattern of increasing attendance for their second-generation members. Between the first and the third generations of the Irish and the French-Canadians, there is evidence of decline in church attendance. And for the Italians and the Spanish-speaking, there is a suggestion that generation has little, if any, influence on going to Mass. If it were not for the inadequate case base for the older generation Spanish-speaking, one might be tempted to argue that the third-generation Mexicans and Puerto Ricans are even less likely to attend formal church services.

At this point, it is important to claim the relevance of ethnicity as a factor in the study of religious behavior. Generational background does not have the universal structural influence it is often presumed to have for all Catholic Americans. Given the already high church involvement of the immigrant Irish and French-Canadians, it would seem most unlikely to find church-going any more frequent among their children and grandchildren. One might expect at most, under the Herberg hypothesis, a continuation of the traditional ties in the third generation. Instead, it is possible to talk of the influence of generational residence in America as diminishing the intensity of Irish and French-Canadian religiousness, rather than maintaining or increasing it.

It is also possible to talk about persisting indifference, in the case of the endogamous Italians and Spanish-speaking. This may well be related to the residential habits of the second and third generations among these groups. The survey does not offer information on the ethnic composition of the neighborhood, but it is reasonable to point out the possibility that persisting ethnic communities, as described for the Italians of Boston by Herbert Gans (1962) or those of New York by Nathan Glazer and Daniel Patrick Moynihan (1970) or of the Mexicans of the Southwest (Grebler, Moore, and Guzman, 1970, pp. 271-289) would reinforce traditional ethnic values and cultural orientations toward religion, even into the third generation and beyond.[6]

The behavior of the German, Polish, and Eastern European Catholics reveals no general rejection of immigrant religious culture and no falling away from the traditional styles. For the fathers and mothers of the second generation, there is a clearly defined increase in weekly church attendance. The increase continues even into the third and later generations for the Germans and Eastern Europeans, but not for the Poles. For some reason, there is evidence that church-going declines among the grandchildren of the Polish immigrants, especially for the men.

Of the seven groups shown in Table 31, it is striking that the Lenski finding of increased church attendance by generation is confirmed only by these three particular nationalities. The Catholic population of Detroit, as described by Lenski (1961, p. 30), itself is biased toward these three ethnic backgrounds. The Irish, the French-Canadians, and the Italians are less predominant in that city's Catholic population; the Germans, the Eastern Europeans, and especially the Poles (see the regional discussion in Chapter Two), on the other hand, are considerably more numerous and may well have comprised the majority of Detroit's Catholic sample in the Lenski study. This discovery in Table 31 would then easily explain Lenski's findings.

A certain broad pattern emerges, given the traditional level of religious involvement of each of the ethnic groups of the first generation. The two most involved nationalities—the Irish and the French-Canadians—are apparently subject to an "Americanized" modification of their religioethnic behavior. The intensity of their religiousness is softened during the American experience.

The three groups at intermediate levels of church-going in the first generation—the Germans, the Poles, and the Eastern Europeans—are perhaps the most likely candidates for an increased involvement. As foreign language groups within the Church, they are subject to the prevailing influence of the Irish-run American Catholic Church, and the influence may take the form of an increase in church attendance among the second generation. Contrary to the notion that the children of the immigrants, as a generalized social category, are ready to reject certain aspects of their ethnic culture, it may well be that the German, Polish, and Eastern European Catholics are eager to become acculturated *within* the Church. Their model for acculturation is the English-speaking Irish, whose involvement in the religion is both traditional and visible.

The Italians and the Spanish-speaking, on the other hand, show relatively little change over generations. Their indifference to formal religion seems to persist, despite the greater religious activity of their fellow Catholics.[7] Part of the explanation may be found in the nature of the persisting ethnic community in the United States, as already suggested. At any rate, the traditional religious indifference and passivity of Italians, Puerto Ricans, and Mexicans is less subject to change (e.g., the influences toward increased formal religiousness) than are the high involvement and association of the Irish and the French-Canadians (e.g., the influences toward becoming less intense). Further explanation and a discussion of these issues, deriving from past history of religion and nationality, are offered in Chapter Six.

Before continuing with this analysis of the traditional religious behavior of the parents, consider testing the Herberg and Lenski three-generation hypotheses on the respondents themselves. Table 32 offers the data for the respondents' attendance at weekly Mass, with controls for ethnicity and generation.

The patterns obtained from the respondents substantiate the patterns reported for their parents. As before, the total figures again confirm the Lenski finding for Catholics in Detroit; with no control for ethnic background, Catholic Americans show increasing frequency in church attendance the longer their families have been in this country. And again, reflecting the ethnic composition of Detroit and the Middle West region, Catholics of German, Polish, and Eastern European origins also show consistent gains in church involvement in second and later generations.

The Irish show some suggestion of a falling away in Mass attendance, and the French-Canadians are the only group to reflect Herberg's expectation of a second-generation decline and then some gain in the third generation. Like the Irish, however, the French-Canadians of the third and later generations do not display the same church-going regularity that characterizes the Irish and French-Canadians who have just recently emigrated to this country.

Table 32. Respondent's Church Attendance by Ethnicity and Generation (Per Cent at Weekly Mass Attendance)

Ethnicity	Respondent's Generation in the United States		
	First	Second	Third or Later
French-Canadian	94	75	83
	(18)	(68)	(58)
Irish	88	80	84
	(16)	(60)	(152)
Italian	72	66	67
	(25)	(235)	(48)
Polish	60	80	79
	(5)[a]	(107)	(48)
Eastern European	53	72	79
	(17)	(108)	(28)
German	50	83	93
	(10)	(70)	(135)
Spanish-speaking	47	42	50
	(47)	(43)	(12)
Total	65	71	82
	(139)	(699)	(484)

$$N = 1,322$$
Non-Catholic spouses = 175
NAP ethnicity = 49
NAP generation = 26
NA attendance — 3

Total = 1,575[b]

[a] Too few cases for adequate percentaging.
[b] The total N of 1,575 is the sum of all born Catholics with Catholic parents; see Table 2.

If any pattern emerges for the Italians, Puerto Ricans, and Mexicans, among these respondents, it is one of persisting indifference: their church attendance in the third generation is no different from that in the first.

Thus there is confirmed evidence of ethnic variation with regard to this aspect of religiocultural behavior. The Lenski findings are consistent only when the ethnic factor is ignored, and the Herberg speculation is not supported at all when ethnicity is controlled. With regard to Hansen's historical interpretation of the social and cultural behavior of immigrants and their descendants, there is no empirical evidence here that could be said to support it. A partial explanation of this problem, given the assumption of accuracy in Hansen's interpretation, might be found in the differences of historically bound epochs of American social history. The rejection of some portions of immigrant culture by the second generation might have been truer of the nineteenth century than the twentieth or the first third of the twentieth century than the more recent decades. The respondents and their parents are reporting their religious behavior for the present and recent past, a period in which the children of immigrants may be experiencing less marginality or cultural dissonance; the nineteenth century and decades up to the depression of the 1930s may have been a time of still greater intergenerational conflict, brought about by the immediacy and onset of social and cultural change, and more profound hostilities between the new Americans and the native population.

A second explanation may be simply the fact that ethnic groups themselves have variations in change, that their different cultures do not all respond to the influences of American society in the same way. Perhaps empirical evidence would find patterns of decline-and-rise among the second- and third-generation Scandinavians in the Middle West at earlier periods in history. Or perhaps this phenomenon might be characteristic of Eastern European Jews in the cities of the Eastern seaboard. If so, these patterns need not necessarily be true for all groups.[8] In any event, it is important to emphasize the persistence of ethnicity for contemporary Catholic Americans not only with regard to differences in religious behavior, but also with patterns of change over generational time.

SOCIAL CLASS AND RELIGIOUS BEHAVIOR

In addition to the factor of generation, one may also suppose that ethnic diversity in religious behavior is a reflection of the class system. In other words, the more frequent religious activity of certain ethnic groups could be explained by the fact that they are characterized in this parental generation by higher levels of education and greater proportions of white-collar workers. The data of Chapter Two demonstrated extensive ethnic diversity in education and occupation. Since it has been observed that the better educated and the white-collar Americans, those with the symbols of higher social and economic status, are also the more likely to involve themselves in voluntary religious activity, some clarification may be found with the control for social class (Pin, 1956; Wickham, 1957; Lenski, 1961).

Tables 33 and 34 offer controls for class and generation. It is clear that socioeconomic status (as measured on the Duncan occupational scalar) does not have the degree of influence that generation has. This is evident both for mothers, as seen in Table 33, and for fathers, shown in Table 34. The only group for which status background is consistently important are the Irish; regardless of generation, the middle- and upper-class Irish are more likely to get to church on Sunday than are the lower-class Irish.

Furthermore, the patterns previously discussed persist. Both for mothers and fathers of the immigrant generation, regardless of class background, the Irish and the French-Canadians are the most involved in church attendance. The Germans, Poles, and other Eastern Europeans comprise an intermediate group, and the Italians, Mexicans, and Puerto Ricans make up the least involved.

Table 33. Mother's Church Attendance by Ethnicity, Generation, and Socio-economic Status (Per Cent at Weekly Mass Attendance)

Ethnicity	First Generation		Second or Later Generation	
	Low SES (1–2)	High SES (3–10)	Low SES (1–2)	High SES (3–10)
French-Canadian	97 (38)	95 (19)	82 (34)	82 (22)
Irish	91 (22)	100 (24)	82 (34)	91 (82)
German	86 (29)	78 (27)	90 (71)	98 (41)
Polish	78 (55)	77 (26)	84 (37)	85 (27)
Eastern European	70 (71)	76 (34)	96 (23)	63 (8)[a]
Italian	67 (112)	76 (110)	71 (34)	70 (43)
Spanish-speaking	56 (62)	65 (23)	65 (17)	33 (6)[a]
Total	73 (390)	79 (264)	83 (257)	84 (238)

$$N = 1,149$$
DK attendance = 27
NA attendance = 4
NA occupation = 11
DK generation = 3

Total = 1,194

[a] Too few cases for adequate percentaging.

Table 34. Father's Church Attendance by Ethnicity, Generation, and Socioeconomic Status (Per Cent at Weekly Mass Attendance)

Ethnicity	First Generation		Second or Later Generation	
	Low SES (1–2)	High SES (3–10)	Low SES (1–2)	High SES (3–10)
French-Canadian	95	78	71	71
	(37)	(18)	(34)	(24)
Irish	82	89	66	83
	(22)	(28)	(32)	(76)
Polish	78	66	81	77
	(60)	(32)	(31)	(22)
German	74	69	88	90
	(31)	(29)	(67)	(39)
Eastern European	59	68	83	80
	(75)	(37)	(18)	(5)[a]
Spanish-speaking	41	31	9	50
	(66)	(26)	(11)	(4)[a]
Italian	40	39	27	38
	(125)	(127)	(15)	(26)
Total	59	55	71	74
	(417)	(297)	(215)	(206)

$$N = 1,135$$
DK attendance = 40
NA attendance = 4
NA occupation = 12
DK generation = 3

Total = 1,194

[a] Too few cases for adequate percentaging.

Moving over into the second and later generations, the pattern of the first generation changes. Among the descendants of the immigrants, the Germans, Poles, and Eastern Europeans exchange places with the traditionally highly involved Irish and French-Canadians: The former groups rise in involvement, whereas the latter groups decline. The place of the Italians and the Spanish-speaking, acknowledging some very small case bases in this sample, tends to stay constant. Class background does not alter the generational pattern.

In all of these percentage-point gains and declines, it is important to emphasize that although the differences are not of staggering magnitude, their directions are fairly consistent. And, too, the decline of involvement among the later generation Irish and French-Canadians in church attendance should not be read to mean a growing tide of apostacy or even marginality among these Catholics. The proportions of weekly church-goers among the Irish and the French-Canadians are still the majority of their groups. The declines merely move these groups away from the high extremity of church association of the immigrant generations, and they are a sign of socioreligious change in accommodation to the cultural atmosphere of the United States.

Before a more detailed account is offered of ethnicity and religion, further confirmation of this pattern would be desirable. If generation in America has the influence it is shown to have for the church attendance of these ethnic groups, then it might be expected to work similar changes with regard to the parochial school system. Irish and French-Canadian parents of the second and later generations might be expected to be less supportive of the Catholic schools. German, Polish, and Eastern European Catholics might be assumed to be more supportive as generation increases. And Italians, Puerto Ricans, and Mexicans, it is hypothesized, would continue to show relatively little support.

Table 35 offers the data for these questions, with controls for the availability of parochial schools and for both generation and class background. There is confirmation in the expected behavior of second-generation Irish and French-Canadians; regardless of socioeconomic position, the 90–100 per cent range of support among those of immigrant background falls to a proportion of around 80 per cent for the later generations. It is interesting to point out here that even the poorest among the Irish and French-Canadian immigrants found the means and had the inclination to send their children to the private school system the Church provided. The evidence here for their support is overwhelming.

The only other ethnic group to offer nearly comparable involvement are the Poles, 86 per cent of those from lower-class immigrant backgrounds sending their children to parochial elementary schools. Because of the already high support among the Polish Catholics in the school system, at least at the elementary school level, there is no appreciable change for later generations.

For the German Catholics, class background appears to make some difference; the middle- and upper-class Germans of both generations are more likely to send their children to available Catholic schools. But generation appears to be even more influential for the Germans. The older generation German Catholics are among the more frequent supporters of the parochial school system.

The case bases for the older generation Eastern Europeans and the Spanish-speaking are too small for any inferences on their behavior here,

Table 35. Parental Support of Catholic Elementary Schools by Ethnicity, Generation, and Socioeconomic Status (Per Cent Sending Respondent to Parochial School)

| | Per Cent with Some or All Catholic Elementary Schooling | | | |
| | First Generation | | Second or Later Generation | |
Ethnicity	Low SES (1–2)	High SES (3–10)	Low SES (1–2)	High SES (3–10)
French-Canadian	97	100	81	81
	(34)	(15)	(27)	(21)
Irish	94	96	82	84
	(16)	(25)	(28)	(64)
Polish	86	92	77	90
	(51)	(24)	(22)	(21)
Eastern European	66	73	57	100
	(50)	(22)	(14)	(5)[a]
German	60	72	82	94
	(15)	(18)	(39)	(32)
Italian	29	43	25	33
	(86)	(96)	(12)	(21)
Spanish-speaking	28	50	67	0
	(39)	(16)	(6)[a]	(4)[a]
Total	59	64	74	79
	(292)	(216)	(154)	(177)

$$N = 839$$
No Catholic school available = 339
No schooling = 3
NA schooling = 1
NA occupation = 9
DK generation = 3

Total = 1,194

[a] Too few cases for adequate percentaging.

but the expected indifference of the Italian Catholics persists over generations. Class background has some effect for both generations of Italians, with the higher status Italians being more supportive of the schools. Socioeconomic position appears to have considerable influence as well for the immigrant generation Mexicans and Puerto Ricans.

SUMMARY

In conclusion, two major facts have emerged in this chapter. First, the diversity in religious behavior, as reflected in church attendance and parochial school support, is an ethnic reality among the immigrant generation of Catholic Americans. And second, the influence of generational experience in the United States on religious behavior is variable, depending not as much on the impact of the American society and culture as on the religioethnic system of the group itself. The Herberg hypothesis is not applicable to different ethnic backgrounds, and Lenski's findings of increased church attendance with longer residence in the United States are confirmed only by total figures for *all* Catholics, but not for all specific ethnic groups.

The ethnic factor has been so vital to different behavioral patterns that such a "law" as the principle of generational differences is really not possible in the pluralism that has been developing in America. The structure of the United States has never been that all-encompassing, that overriding, that total to warrant easy generalizations about changing ethnic behavior. There are too many exceptions to talk about uniform regularities. The black experience in historical America and in contemporary years and the American Indian experience, both of which we are just beginning to understand in terms of ethnicity and pluralism, have told us that much.

Above all, it is difficult to expect symmetrical behavior over time from three generations of different ethnic groups, not only because there are cultural variations among the diverse ethnic backgrounds themselves, but also because the societal influences keep changing, and different ethnic groups (collectively and individually) encounter their third generations in America at different times. The concept "third generation" has often been interpreted to be a kind of coming of cultural age in America, but the grandchildren of the immigrants experience their third generations in vastly different settings, in the largest cities and the isolated prairies, in diverse regions and sectors, under conditions of rising affluence and entrenched poverty, in static, depressed, and opportunity-rich economies, and, above all, at different times and under different, changing, American norms. Together with fundamental ethnic diversity to begin with, it is not at all surprising that the concept "third generation" means different things to different groups.

The following chapter will deal with and explain the broader question of diversity in terms of various religioethnic systems: the historical development of the unique characteristics within Catholicism which differentiate ethnic groups in the United States. Subsequently, Chapter Seven will examine the religious behavior of the respondent's own generation, rather than that of his parents, and will focus on the extent of change which comes from ethnic exogamy, or the dissolution of the ethnic family, as well as that which results from length of residence in the United States.

NOTES

1.   The historical works of Marcus Hansen and Oscar Handlin are an essential beginning in the study of immigration. Numerous sociological writings are available, but these are typically descriptive rather than analytical. The better sociological studies of immigrant life appear as studies of communities, as discussed in Chapter One. See, for example, Anderson (1938) and Ware (1935), and especially the perceptions and insights at the height of mass immigration in Woods (1903).

2.   This study is confined to an examination of ritual involvement and associational behavior, the extent of religiousness as indicated by external forms, such as Mass attendance, Communion, and parochial school support. Thus religiousness is defined, as in Lenski's (1961, pp. 18–24) distinction of commitment, by the associational dimension of ritual involvement, rather than by the communal level of primary group relationships with one's coreligionists, or by subjective piety. The communal aspect of religion is implicit in this study, inasmuch as interethnic marriage, as defined, is that which occurs within the same religion.

3.   Evidence for the extent of reliability of the respondents' reporting of parental religious behavior is positive. See Greeley and Rossi (1966, p. 44).

4.   The more well-known aspect of Catholic ethnic diversity in religious behavior is the Irish-Italian comparison in the United States. Among many who have observed this phenomenon are Cole (1903) at the turn of the century and, more recently in the same city (Boston) that Cole reported on, Gans (1962, pp. 110–115). See also Lopreato (1970, pp. 87–93). The contrast between the Irish and the Italian variants of Catholicism is also often mentioned in many works of fiction. A recent novel, *Principato*, by Tom McHale (1970), is a fascinating depiction of the Catholic subculture of Philadelphia. The novel symbolizes in a very personalized manner the Italian indifference to the formal Church and the intense Catholicity of the Irish. The disparity is stark, between the "Defiance" of the Italians and the rigid Jansenism of the Irish.

5. There is a hint here that the religious involvement of the spouse plays an important role in the influence of one's own level of religious association. And because these data refer only to endogamous parents, there is the suggestion that the nature of ethnic attachments (to spouse and, presumably, to group) do indeed bear some weight on religious behavior. This would be consistent with the anthropological idea that endogamy is a contributor to cultural and religious continuity. I shall return to these notions in Chapter Seven.

6. Among others, Lieberson (1963) has documented the segregation patterns of ethnic groups over time in American urban centers. More recently, Kantrowitz (1969) has shown the persistence of some ethnic residential enclaves in New York, particularly those of the Italians and the Scandinavians.

7. Russo (1968, 1970) presents data on the religious behavior of three generations of Italians in New York City and argues the case for increased involvement of Italian Catholics within the Church. This is consistent with Lenski's findings, but it disputes Herberg's thesis of some rejection of tradition by the second generation. Close examination of Russo's data suggest, however, that the Italians of New York are becoming more similar to the Irish in terms of *informal* religious practice, but they are not becoming more involved in attendance at Mass or reception of Communion.

8. And, finally, another explanation may stem from the neglect of ethnic research. The third-generation hypothesis may relate to the fact that originally it was primarily the educated among ethnic groups who experienced a rejection of traditional ethnic culture, and that the rank-and-file of ethnic memberships never actually went through this stage. For the better educated, the intellectuals, and the professionals there may have been embarrassment at being marginal between the groups into which they were born and the larger American society, and some turning away from the ethnic past was the result produced. If so, this phenomenon was more likely to be evident among the better educated and be understood more sharply by those in a position to write about it. It may never have extended very prominently into the lower status segments of American ethnic groups. If this is plausible, a very refined social class measure (which is capable of differentiating the intellectuals and professionals from the middle and lower classes) is necessary for an empirical test. For other discussions of the third-generation hypothesis, see Lazerwitz and Rowitz (1964) and Bender and Kagiwada (1968).

CHAPTER SIX

THE CULTURES OF CATHOLICISM: TOWARD THE SOCIOLOGY OF RELIGIOETHNIC SYSTEMS

The Catholicism of Mediterranean countries, as well as of Ireland, is rooted not so much in the ethnic character of the peoples as in historical conditions, which, however influenced by ethnic factors, have been subject also to other and more decisive influences . . . Perhaps religion is as often responsible for ethnic character as the latter is responsible for the faith.

H. RICHARD NIEBUHR (1929)

THE HISTORICAL AND SOCIOLOGICAL FACT of ethnic diversity within religion is well known. Church scholars have often incorporated the phenomenon into discourses on the social history of religion (Niebuhr, 1957; Latourette, 1958–1962). Historians of nationalism have examined the role of religion in the sociopolitical movements of European peoples and have pointed out the dissonant or consonant relationships of ethnic minorities with religious institutions (Kolarz, 1946; Kohn, 1956; Baron, 1960; Deutsch, 1966). And sociologists have sometimes examined different social systems in terms of religious or ethnic conflict (Wirth, 1945; Cahnman, 1964).[1]

From the comparative point of view, however, the sociological and historical analysis of religion and ethnicity has been much neglected. A problem for sociology is the understanding of elements that contribute to the shape of religious behavior, and the search for meaningful social and cultural patterns among the welter of historical facts.[2] The exploration of the roots of ethnic diversity within a common religion affords this kind of opportunity for sociological and historical research.

The evidence of ethnic diversity within the Catholic Church presented in preceding chapters raises a number of questions. What are the structural sources of the religious traditions that the different immigrant groups brought with them to America? What religious and national characteristics help explain these distinctive levels of ethnic involvement among the foreign-born Catholics in the United States? Considerable research has been done on individual ethnic backgrounds, and some of this is cited in this book, but what comparative analysis can be employed for all six ethnic backgrounds of concern in this chapter: Irish, French-Canadian, Italian, Mexican and Puerto Rican, Polish, and German?[3]

Comparison is developed around a model of societal competition, based on the social and political characteristics of national Catholicism in the histories of these six American ethnic groups. The research is necessarily limited in a number of different ways. A good deal of religious involvement certainly is to be explained by social-psychological factors, such as an individual's subjective ethnic identification, cultural and religious value systems, and the nature of national character. The following model does not dwell on the psychological determinants of religious association as much as on the more sociological and political factors contributing to the shape of religioethnicity.

127

Furthermore, the emphasis, consistent with the discussion in Chapter Five, is placed on formal religious association and involvement, and not on "religiosity" or the measure of religious experience, feeling, or piety. The distinction is between that which is public, formal, and integrated into Church requirements and that which is private, informal, and at variance with Church norms.

A third point refers to the factor of immigration. The investigation is limited to the traditional sources of the old country, the historical origins presumed to give rise to traits and values brought to America with immigration. I am assuming that an understanding of the roots of ethnicity is important and basic for ongoing study into the changes brought about by the American experience. Finally, the research is limited by reliance on the secondary literature. Perhaps future efforts in social history and the sociology of religion and ethnicity will survey primary sources in developing our knowledge of comparative ethnic behavior.

THE NATURE OF SOCIETAL COMPETITION

There may be numerous approaches for explaining the differential religious involvement of Catholic groups, but one of the common problems is the lack of empirical data with which to make a systematic beginning. In this regard, an important contribution to the comparative study of religious behavior is Michael Fogarty's *Christian Democracy in Western Europe* (1957), for its valuable work on socioreligious movements.

Fogarty (1957, p. 7) is concerned with associational involvement within Protestantism and Catholicism. "Across Western Europe from Flanders to Venice, there lies a belt of high religious observance, where people are more likely than elsewhere not only to profess a religion but to practice it; a sort of heartland of European Christianity." With concern for the imperfect statistics of religious practice, Fogarty (1957, p. 7) tentatively argues that this phenomenon might be traced, as in the frequency of Protestant religious observance in Germany, to the nature of religious competition and the proportions of different religions in the population:

One explanation might be that religion thrives on competition, since the areas of low observance tend also to be those where the proportion of Protestants in the total population is highest. Silesia, an eastern territory, but one where the balance between Catholics and Protestants was till the Second World War more equal than elsewhere, showed till then a rather high level of observance among Protestants. But if there is such a rule it should apply also to Catholics, whereas in fact the statistics show that Catholic observance is high in the mainly Catholic west and south, but falls away, like observance among Protestants, toward the mainly Protestant east and north.

Thus, within Germany, the relationship between high observance and the viability of religious competition does not seem to hold for German Catholics. Fogarty (1957, p. 8) pursues this further, with an examination of the more specific geographical outlines of the "heartland" of practicing Christianity, both Catholic and Protestant:

High observance . . . is most commonly to be found in the belt, which includes Holland, Belgium, French Flanders, Alsace-Lorraine, Westfalia, the Rhineland, most of south Germany and Austria, Switzerland (although here statistics are lacking), and parts of north Italy. There are large Protestant as well as Catholic populations in this area, and the tendency to high observance applies to both. As the case of Germany shows, competition between religions is probably not by itself enough to explain this. But it may be that competition of a more general kind is at the bottom of it; for this is a land not only of political but also of linguistic and cultural frontiers.

Fogarty stops here with this particular hypothesis, but the idea of linguistic and cultural competition might well be developed as a basic dimension of the level of religious involvement. Indeed, had Fogarty considered the cases of Ireland and Quebec (which were excluded from his survey of Western Europe), the argument for the influence of cultural competition on religious observance would have assumed even stronger tones.

The concept of societal competition, whether political-linguistic or political-cultural, is a relevant one for the sociology of religioethnic systems. As Fogarty suggests in the case of Germany, mere religious heterogeneity within a society is not sufficient for explaining levels of religious involvement. More to the point is the proximity to and the salience of religious and cultural differences within the ethnic orientation of a people. Thus the idea of the frontier between competing groups serves as a symbol of competition and diversity, especially if the frontier represents a border separating the powerful from the powerless.

The idea of societal competition then embraces at least two specific macrosociological factors. The first is the presence of religious differences, reinforced by linguistic and cultural competition. The extent of conflict generated by the competition may vary, but there is always some sense of competition. It is reasonable to suppose that the greater the conflict, the more salient the sense of religious distinctiveness and the higher the level of religious involvement for the competitively subordinate group.

A second major factor refers to the degree of political autonomy enjoyed by the cultural groups involved. Competition between religioethnic systems might be present within the borders of the same geographical area, or the competition might be an expression of distinctiveness across frontiers. Political control by a different religioethnic group may be present within the given society (as a kind of internal colonialism), or it may extend across geographical borders (in the classic conventions of external colonialism).[4] In either event, the reality of societal competition is expected to reflect differences in political power and autonomy between the cultural groups.

Following fairly closely from Fogarty's suggestion, the model of societal competition is based on two dimensions: (1) differences in religiocultural systems and (2) differences in their political power. Other points might well be taken into consideration. Religioethnic distinctiveness in the past has often led to nationalist movements, and the institutionalization of religioethnic differences under certain conditions may lead to political movements of secession and independence (Wirth, 1945). These movements reinforce religious consciousness along with other aspects of cultural identity. The converse of this relationship may also be true. Emergent nationalism may stimulate dormant religioethnic distinctiveness, and the new consciousness then reinforces the political movement.

Other, more microsociological factors are presumably relevant in the context of societal competition. The extent of religiocommunal organization, the relationship of religion to the needs of the people, and the extent to which there is conflict of class interests within the given religioethnic group are some of the important questions, and they will be considered in the subsequent analysis.

It is generally proposed then that the condition of societal competition, with its characteristics of religioethnic differences, conflict, and corresponding levels of power, is a positive correlate of the degree of religioethnic activity and consciousness. A review of the state of Catholicity in the background histories of six American ethnic groups will document the degree of societal competition experienced by these peoples and should help explain their varied levels of involvement within their shared religion.[5]

THE IRISH

Perhaps the greatest difficulty which confronts the historian of the Irish is that of differentiating between the specifically Irish and specifically Catholic aspects of their lives. They had emerged into the modern world from a past in which Catholicism had played a stronger role than among any other people of Western Europe.

THOMAS N. BROWN (1966)

The fusion of religion and nationality, inherent in the foregoing quotation from Thomas Brown (1966, pp. 34–35), is perhaps the most recurrent theme in the meaning of Irish ethnicity. The fusion was the consequence of centuries of societal competition with the Protestant English. For the Irish the competition meant conflict, and the conflict itself was virtually institutionalized within the structure of the society. It incorporated every aspect of life, including religion.

In her history and accounting of the Irish famine of the 1840s, Cecil Woodham-Smith (1962) provides a background to the English rule in Ireland and discusses the proscriptions of the Penal Laws dating from 1695. The Penal Code was not completely repealed until 1829 (Catholic emancipation), and for well over a century the laws were intended for "the destruction of Catholicism in Ireland" (Woodham-Smith, 1962, p. 27):

> In broad outline, they barred Catholics from the army and navy, the law, commerce, and from every civic activity. No Catholic could vote, hold any office under the Crown, or purchase land, and Catholic estates were dismembered by an enactment directing that at the death of the Catholic owner his land was to be divided among all his sons, unless the eldest became a Protestant, when he would inherit the whole. Education was made almost impossible.... The practice of the Catholic faith was proscribed; informing was encouraged as "an honourable service" and priest-hunting treated as a sport. Such were the main provisions of the Penal Code, described by Edmund Burke as "a machine as well fitted for the oppression, impoverishment and degradation of a people, and the debasement in them of human nature itself, as ever proceeded from the perverted ingenuity of man."

Irish Catholicism thus was inevitably different from the Church in France, Spain, or Italy. Religion in Ireland did not mean vested interests, the dilemmas of institutionalization, or priorities in whatever established society there happened to be to the degree that religion on the Continent did. Far longer in history, the Church in Ireland had been poor, landless, and without power. It was more objectively and subjectively an integral part of the peasant's own poverty, and it could not be held responsible for the problems of such poverty. It shared a subordinate status, and this fact facilitated the identification the individual Irishman made of his struggling religion with his struggling nationality.

The Irish had no prevailing class of prosperous clergy to contrast with the poverty of the peasants; instead, many Irish priests were close to and among the people. The closing of the monasteries threw the friars out to beg among the poor. Sean O'Faolain (1949) writes of the rebellious strain among the clergy when, in the period 1805 to 1845, the forces of O'Connellism in the presbytery were fighting and defeating the monarchists and their traditions of Gallicanism in the seminary, or even more actively, in still earlier years, when priests either died with guns in their hands during the 1798 Rebellion or were taken to be hanged after the Rising ended.[6]

George Potter (1960) notes that the fusion of religion and nationality was so complete in Irish Catholic culture that it extended even to their linguistic view of the English. The Irish word *Sassenach*, for example, means both Protestant and Englishman. Apostacy from Catholicism was considered the greatest of crimes in the sight of the Irish peasant; the apostate was thought to be a betrayer not only of religion, but also of nationality (Potter, 1960, pp. 71, 75–83). This is an excellent example of what Vladimir Nahirny and Joshua Fishman (1966, p. 328), in another context, have called the far-reaching syncretism of ethnic and religious values and traditions: culminating in the "sanctification" of ethnicity and the "ethnization" of religion.

Thus much of Irish Catholicism was a response to the societal competition confronting the people. There was always England, identified with contempt and hate, trying to Anglicize Ireland and proscribe everything Irish, including the Irish religion. The persecution fostered the integration of the nationality with the religion and contributed a great deal to the emergence of the feelings of nationalism.

Glazer (1954) has remarked how the Irish Catholic immigrants in the United States were more likely to identify themselves first as being from Ireland, rather than Galway or Cork, as opposed to the Italian Catholics, whose lack of national consciousness had them view their primary origins as Sicily or Calabria (or even villages and communes within these regions), instead of Italy. The choice of local or national identification probably has much to do with the extent of religioethnic involvement and degree of societal competition.

The question of national identification should not be confused with the ideology of nationalism. National identification developed around anti-English themes and was probably much more pervasive than the reality of nationalism, with its complicated sets of opposing issues and directions.[7] The movement for nationalism, however, was based upon the foundation of societal competition and gathered much of its strength and logic from the argument for religioethnic distinctiveness.[8]

The history of societal competition, with its elements of religioethnic conflict and corresponding facts of Irish powerlessness, contributed a good deal to the shape of Irish Catholicity.[9] It was a heritage developed in Ireland and represented quite clearly by the Irish immigrants in the United States, not only in the development of the structure of the Catholic Church in

America but also in their high level of association with and involvement in its religious requirements.

THE FRENCH-CANADIANS

The religious element was never absent from the second Hundred Years' War which the French and English waged against each other in America until the downfall of New France. This fact has left its mark on the French-Canadian mentality, which weds the concept of nationality to that of religion and asserts its separateness from English-speaking North America on both counts.

MASON WADE (1946)

This historical accounting of the French-Canadians by Mason Wade (1946, p. 22) suggests the important similarity shared with the Irish: the interpenetration of religion and nationality in confrontation with the Protestant English-speaking Canadians. The parallels with the Irish in terms of societal competition are striking, especially for the similar end results of extremely close association with the religious and educational life of the Catholic Church.

Despite general similarity, the Catholic history of the French-Canadians is unique in some ways, and this has contributed a more tradition-based, parochial social organization to French-Canadian religious affairs. The French in Canada never experienced the degree of devastation of their society and culture the Irish did. Although the different views of the relationship between Church and State have caused political conflicts in Canada, the French-Canadians in Quebec had geographical insularity and enough sovereignty for the elaborate development of a parish-dominated social organization.

The problems of conflict and powerlessness, as well as a resultant nationalism, are explicit in the bilingual and bicultural consciousness that characterizes contemporary Canada.[10] They are expressed in the separatist movement in Quebec and have come to prevail in much of the analysis of French-Canadian society and culture. Quoting Marcel Rioux, Fernand Dumont (1965, p. 392) offers a summary of the national character:

"The French-Canadian ideology has always rested on three characteristics of the French-Canadian culture—the fact that it is a minority culture, that it is Catholic, and that it is French. It is from these characteristics, first envisaged concretely but, with the passing of time, more and more as a framework, that ideology has formulated its national doctrine and has come to control the thinking of most of the educational and intellectual institutions of Quebec." As can be seen, here again the Conquest has not been forgotten.

The distinctiveness of societal competition rests as much with economic disparity as it does with the question of political power. Much has been written about the conscious and unconscious confinement of French-Canadian resources (Rioux and Martin, 1965). The "second-class citizenship" qualities which are perceived to arise from the ethnic division of labor in Canada are not unlike some of the economic and social problems between blacks and whites in the United States.

Although similar in kind if not intensity to the religioethnic conflicts of the Irish and the English, historical experiences in Quebec have allowed the Church to take advantage of opportunities for its development. In his review of the place of Catholicism in French Canada, Jean-Charles Falardeau (1965, p. 342) notes that from the beginning of its settlement, Quebec society has been completely surrounded by and dominated by the influence of Catholicism: "The history of French Canada is the history of the Church in Canada and vice versa."

Tied to the notions of the church and society are the two central themes of language and nationalism. The French language is more than a medium of communication or a carrier of culture in Quebec. It is almost mystically regarded as the "guardian of the faith." As another instance of the "sanctification" of ethnicity, the loss of language is believed frequently to lead to the loss of Catholicism, and the depth of this conviction has led to the elaborate development of the parochial school system not only in Quebec, but also among the American children of the French-Canadian immigrants in New England (Falardeau, 1965; Lemaire, 1966).

The politicoreligious philosophy of French-Canadian nationalism has also gained explicit and widespread support among clergy and laymen alike. "This was the belief in French Canada's fortunate vocation based on one obvious sign—the fact that modern France, in becoming secular and atheistic, had abandoned its mission as the older daughter of the Church, while the French-Canadians had remained faithful to the past and to God, and must therefore replace a France who had betrayed its trust" (Falardeau, 1965, pp. 350–351). The intensity of this feeling, as exemplified by the involvement and association of French-Canadians with their religion, is evident.

In terms of the more microsociological aspects of religion in the French-Canadian community, the pervasive Catholicity stands out still more sharply. In his discussion of the growth of industry and the changes in the economic and social order of French Canada, Everett Hughes (1963, p. 10) points out how the parish persists as the central aspect of the French-Canadian's life: "The parish was historically the first institution of local self-government in rural Quebec; it remains the point of active integration of religious and secular matters. The roles of parishioner and of citizen are scarcely distinguishable."

The role of religion in the daily routine of rural Quebec is so predominant as to comprise in itself the meaning of communality. In his account of St. Denis, Horace Miner (1939, p. 105) observes the Mass to be so important to the social system of the parish that he devotes an entire chapter to the effect it has on village life: "Masses are public religious celebrations whether they are Sunday Masses or Masses for marriages, anniversaries of death, burial, or special supplication. They are practically the only activity in which the whole parish participates as a group."

The clergy of Quebec are an essential part of this communality. Like the priests of Ireland, they share similar backgrounds and values with their parishioners. The historical pattern is important because it means that the clergy of French Canada have rarely been recruited from a single social class, let alone a dominant status, in contrast to the custom of many European countries. "One seldom finds a French-Canadian family that does not include a member or a relative who is in the clergy or in one of the orders," writes Falardeau (1965, p. 355).[11] The clergy are within and of all strata of the society.

The traditions of Quebec province were transplanted in New England by the French-Canadians who immigrated, and the transplanting was an easier task because of the proximity to Canada. They concentrated almost exclusively on the reestablishment of the parish-centered social organization (Theriault, 1960; Lemaire, 1966). On the communication between the two countries, Jacques Ducharme (1943, p. 14) writes: "By visit and by letter a sort of communal life exists. Birth and marriage and death are the interest of all, and the frontier is no barrier, for it merely serves to separate the clans temporarily."

In his fictional representation of French-Canadian life in New England, Ducharme (1939, p. 52) conveys the importance of the religious traditions:

The Church meant a great deal to the French Canadian who had left his country. It was like the hub of a wheel to which he gravitated once a week, and which set his pace. There he could always hear his own language spoken, and there he could find solace in time of trouble. Not yet broken was the spell that the village church had for him when he was on his farm in Quebec.

As with all immigrant groups, there are interests in and attempts at maintaining the traditions of the Old World (Park and Miller, 1921). The Irish and the French-Canadians brought their own distinctive views of religion and styles of group involvement. Because of the extent of cultural and religious conflict and competition within their societies, and their traditions of well-developed communal organizations, each brought to the United States its own intimate association with formal religion. Other Catholic groups had other kinds of historical experiences, and consequently they brought other religious traditions.

THE SOUTHERN ITALIANS

> They unfurled a red-white-and-green handkerchief from the church-tower, they rang the bells in a frenzy, and they began to shout in the village square, "Hurray for liberty!"
>
> Like the sea in storm. The crowd foamed and swayed in front of the club of the gentry, and outside the Town Hall, and on the steps of the church—a sea of white stocking-caps, axes and sickles glittering. Then they burst into the little street.
>
> "Your turn first, baron! You who have had folks cudgelled by your estate-keepers!"
>
> At the head of all the people a witch, with her old hair sticking up, armed with nothing but her nails. "Your turn, priest of the devil! for you've sucked the soul out of us!"
>
> ...Then for his Reverence who used to preach Hell for anybody who stole a bit of bread. He was just coming back from saying mass, with the consecrated Host inside his fat belly. "Don't kill me, I am in mortal sin!" Neighbor Lucia being the mortal sin; Neighbor Lucia whose father had sold her to the priest when she was fourteen years old, at the time of the famine winter, and she had ever since been filling the streets and the Refuge with hungry brats....
>
> GIOVANNI VERGA (1883)

The stories of Giovanni Verga, as well as the novels of other Italian writers, illustrate dramatically the estrangement of the Southern Italians from the Catholic Church.[12] Indeed, the quoted episode goes further than suggesting the contempt of these peasants for the Church; it points to the links between anticlericalism and the nationalist mood.

In stark contrast to the Catholicity of the Irish and the French-Canadians, the state of formal church-involved religiousness in Sicily and other regions of Southern Italy was in a precarious condition, a legacy of the alliance between the Church and the Old Order. The idea and reality of societal competition—that network of conflicts between linguistic and religious differences—were nonexistent in Southern Italy. There was no identification of a populistic religion or church with powerlessness and national identity. The history of the nineteenth century in Italy shows the Catholic Church to be, for the most part, an established force against national consciousness and, directly and indirectly, for maintaining the powerlessness of the poor. In a real sense, the institutional Church was itself the alien religion—the Catholicism of Rome, the North, the upper classes, and the status quo (Jemolo, 1960; Baron, 1960).

From the point of view of the educated classes of the South, the Papacy and the State were one. This helped to produce both anticlericalism and widespread indifference to formal religion, just as the interlocking of religion and nationality helped to create intense identification with Catholicism among the Irish and the French-Canadians. In the Italy of the nineteenth century, resistance or indifference to the social order extended to religion.

The fact that cultural distinctions prevailed between the North and the South of Italy did not change with political unification. Kenneth Latourette (1958, Vol. I, pp. 415–419) notes how important geography was in the structure of the Catholic Church in Italy. It was from the regions north of Rome where most of the active support of the Church could be found. All of the Popes of the nineteenth century were born in the North, with the sole exception of Leo XIII; even he was a native of the region only slightly to the south of Rome. Most of the new congregations had their beginnings in the North. Little activity and even less support could be traced to the *Mezzogiorno*. And it was from the south of Italy that the vast majority of immigrants to the United States had come (Foerster, 1919).

The writings of many scholars, both proclerical and anticlerical in temperament, provide evidence of the popular moods toward religious involvement with formal Catholicism. The struggles between the Church and the movement for unification left their mark, as noted in Henry Browne's (1946) survey of the "Italian problem" within American Catholicism: "The comments of an anti-papal Italian traveller to America suggests that almost of necessity the political affairs of Italy, which for years made it practically impossible for a good Catholic to be a good citizen of the newly united Italy, had an influence on the religious mentality of Italians even after migration."[13]

In his autobiography, Constantine Panunzio (1921, p. 18) describes the memories of his boyhood in Apulia, in a home that can be said to be comfortable, if neither affluent nor impoverished:

> While we all received instruction of various kinds, dealing mainly with good manners and proper conduct, our religious education was very limited, almost a negligible factor in our lives. Religion was considered primarily a woman's function, unnecessary to men, and a matter about which they continually joked. . . . We children

continuously heard our male relatives speak disparagingly of religion, if religion it could be called. They would speak of the corruption of the Church.

Among the poorest classes, educational and religious instruction in formal Catholicism were even less common and characteristic. Feelings against the Church were widespread, if not always vocal. Edward Banfield (1958) describes the lack of both religious and secular influence of the two churches and their priests in Montegrano.[14] Barely more than 10 per cent of the 3400 Montegranesi go to hear Mass on a Sunday, and most of these are women (Banfield, 1958, pp. 17–18):

> By tradition the men of Montegrano are anti-clerical. The tradition goes back a century or more to a time when the church had vast holdings in Southern Italy and was callous and corrupt. Today it owns only one small farm in Montegrano, and the village priests are both known to be kindly and respectable men. Nevertheless priests in general—so many Montegranesi insist—are money-grubbers, hypocrites, and worse.

Despite changes in the social and religious system the feelings had become a tradition. As Ann Cornelisen (1969, p. 292) notes: "The Church's true immorality has been collective. In collusion with feudal landlords, it sapped the vitality of Southern Italy. When it was divested of its holdings in 1870 it was already too late. The process of exhaustion had been gradual but constant." And the tradition of relative indifference to and contempt for the formal Church was brought to the United States with immigration.

It is ironic that the indifference to the formal doctrines of Catholicism among the Southern Italians persisted despite the fact that so many of the *contadini* were fairly isolated in their peasant villages and removed from the currents of anticlericalism and changing political thought abroad throughout Italy. Rudolph Vecoli (1969, p. 228) points out that much of this is due to the particularistic folk-ceremonies of the local varieties of religion:

> While nominally Roman Catholics, theirs was a folk religion, a fusion of Christianity and pre-Christian elements, of animism, polytheism, and sorcery with the sacraments of the Church. . . . Dominated by a sense of awe, fear, and reverence for the supernatural, the peasants were profoundly religious. However, their beliefs and practices did not conform to the doctrines and liturgy of the Church.

This variant of religion, of course, clashed with the more institutional ecclesiasticism of the Vatican, as it clashed after immigration with the Irish style of Catholicism predominant in America (Covello, 1967, pp. 103–145; Vecoli, 1969).

Regardless of the lack of ideological anticlericalism, the poor in Southern Italy, in marked contrast to the poor in Ireland and Quebec, often showed contempt for the formal religion.[15] For this they had the justification of their own experience. Vecoli (1969, p. 229) summarizes this orientation:

> For the Church as an institution the South Italian peasants had little sense of reverence. Historically it had been allied with the land-owning aristocracy and had shown little sympathy for the misery of the *contadini*. Although surrounded by a multitude of clergy, the people by and large were not instructed in the fundamental doctrines of the Catholic faith. Toward their village priests, whom they regarded as parasites living off their labors, the peasants often displayed attitudes of familiar contempt. Clerical immorality and greed figured largely in the folk humor of Italy.

The lack of involvement in the Church in Southern Italy, it is proposed, is due to the comparative absence of societal competition between distinct cultural and religious systems. In Southern Italy Catholicism was identified not with an emerging sense of social and political reform, but with the existing policies of the old order. The characteristics of competition as defined—the extent of religioethnic conflict and the salience of powerlessness—contributed to high Church involvement and religious observance among the Irish and the French-Canadians. Religious and cultural differences were absent in Southern Italy, and the model of competition worked in reverse because it was the Church that was held responsible for social problems and not some foreign cultural system.

THE MEXICANS AND THE PUERTO RICANS

A factor all but universal in Spanish America . . . was the shock brought to the Roman Catholic Church by independence and the inevitably painful adjustments. Crises arose from the disorders which were features of the wars of independence, from the Spanish birth of many of the clergy, from the historic patronage exercised by the crown, from the insistence of new governments on the transfer to them of that authority, from the unwillingness of Madrid to surrender its prerogatives, and from the political situation in Spain which made Rome hesitate to go counter to Spanish claims.

KENNETH SCOTT LATOURETTE (1958–1962)

Societal competition between religious and cultural systems was also lacking in Mexico and Puerto Rico as elsewhere throughout Latin America, and some of the same problems of the history of Church and State in Italy could be seen in the history of Spanish-speaking America. Most notable, as the foregoing quotation suggests (Latourette, 1958–1962, Vol. III, p. 295), is the universality of Church power and control.

To varying extents, Latin American countries were considered as mission territories by the Church. This led to a number of unique factors that were subsequently seen to contribute to the lack of involvement of Latin Americans in the formal religious system of Catholicism. Both Mexico and Puerto Rico emerged from the Spanish colonial tradition, and the attachments of Mexicans and Puerto Ricans to the Church were founded not as much on the basis of instruction and conviction—both positive values of Catholicism—as on the presence of social and religious customs, artifactual medals, holy pictures, and fiestas (Fitzpatrick, 1955).

According to a recent study by François Houtart and Émile Pin (1965), data on the low religious observance of Latin American Catholics form a regular pattern which is traced to and explained by the predominance of the colonial tradition itself. The people of Latin America are ascribed Catholics, and subsequently religion becomes a mere social attribute. Religion then becomes nothing more than another characteristic with which one is born.

The state of Catholicity in Latin America is further affected by the underdeveloped conditions of religiocommunal organization, data for which will be presented at the end of this chapter. The numbers of priests are few relative to the size of the population in Latin America, and parishes are too large and thus inadequate for religious organization.[16] Above all, the clergy were traditionally recruited from Europe during the early years of colonization, in keeping with the missionary perspective of the areas. This only served to maintain the problem of social and religious distance between parishioner and Church.

The distance between the clergy and the people mirrors the broader problems of Church and State. As in Italy, there was no competition with alien cultures and religions. Instead, there was conflict with the established powers of Catholicism. J. Lloyd Mecham (1934) and others (Pike, 1964) have pointed out how much at odds the Church and its Spanish-born clergy were with the movements for political independence. In the subsequent conflicts in the different countries, the clergy were often divided. With few exceptions, the general division saw the bishops and higher clergy standing for the monarchical form of government, and the lower clergy (who were increasingly native-born to Latin America as the societies grew more populous) either inactive or moving on the side of change.

In Mexico, the leadership in the political struggle for independence came at first from the local village priests, who were close to the pressing social problems of the population (Mecham, 1934). In this, as far as the role of the local village priest was concerned, the Mexican struggle was similar to the Irish. The differences for the larger societies, however, are evident. There was less division among the clergy in Ireland, partly because of the overwhelming presence of religious and cultural differences with the English lords. In Mexico, as elsewhere in Latin America, the clergy who did take the side of independence found themselves in a position which the Church hierarchy deplored. It was a classic case of pervasive role conflict. In Spanish America, it was the religiously homogeneous society that was in competition with itself; there was no alien religiocultural scapegoat, real or imagined.

In Puerto Rico too, as throughout much of Latin America, orthodoxy within Catholicism prevailed almost exclusively among the upper classes, very few in number. Despite the Church's standardized doctrines and procedures, local communities in Puerto Rico blended formal Catholicism with cults of saints, witchcraft, spiritualism, and, in the twentieth century, even with elements of Protestantism (Steward, 1956). The fact of variation to the formal religion of Catholicism is not unlike the deviations of folk religion found in the expressive life of Southern Italy.

Julian Steward (1956) draws attention to a number of factors that prevented the integration of the greater proportion of Puerto Ricans into the institutionalized life of the Church. Poverty, dispersal of the population, inadequate clergy, missionary attitudes of patronization, and the inconsistent stands of the Church on social issues (e.g., slavery) all contributed to the shape of religion in Puerto Rico. As in Mexico, there was no historical confrontation for Catholicism in Puerto Rico, and this fact would influence not only the Church's view of Latin Americans but also the population's view of the Church.

After the United States became sovereign over Puerto Rico, there came a complete separation of religion from the government. The island was opened, for the first time, to missionary activity by Protestant groups. Steward argues that these two events introduced still more heterogeneity to the Catholicism of the island, and they even worked to supplant the traditional religious forms in some areas of Puerto Rico.

Studies of Mexican and Puerto Rican communities in the United States document quite consistently the "token bond" with formal Catholicism that characterizes the Spanish-speaking groups (Tuck, 1946; Mills, Senior and Goldsen, 1950; Padilla, 1958; Glazer and Moynihan, 1963; Rubel, 1966; Grebler, Moore, and Guzman, 1970; Fitzpatrick, 1971). Like the Italians, the Mexicans and the Puerto Ricans brought with them to the United States their ethnic indifference to a religious system which they, for the most part, either traditionally took for granted or perceived to be standing in the way of change and needed reform. They differ quite essentially from the Irish and the French-Canadians, for whom the fights for autonomy in matters of nationality and religion substantially reinforced each other.

THE POLISH CATHOLICS

> Religion was . . . in some measure a field of national cooperation, particularly in the southeastern part of Russian Poland, Lithuania, and White Ruthenia, where religious and national interests went hand in hand. . . . But aesthetic and intellectual interests had but little influence upon the large masses of the population and . . . the role of the Catholic Church in Polish national life was limited by its international politics. The most secure and the widest ground of national cooperation lay elsewhere—in the economic domain.
>
> W. I. THOMAS and FLORIAN ZNANIECKI(1927)

The Polish Catholics, like the German Catholics to be discussed next, show a degree of involvement not exactly similar to the four backgrounds already presented. The Poles are indeed fairly involved in their religion, and thus they are decidedly different from the Italians and the Spanish-speaking of Latin America. But given the empirical levels of religious and educational involvement, the Poles do not represent the type of intensity that characterizes the place of the Irish and the French-Canadians in historical and contemporary Catholicism. They reflect a kind of intermediacy.

It is frequently observed that the state of Catholicism in Poland has been historically similar to the religious affairs of Ireland and Quebec. Salo Baron (1960, pp. 96–108) offers Polish history as another instance of the coincidence of national interests and religious loyalties. Vladimir Nahirny and Joshua Fishman (1966) discuss the presumed consequences of ethnic and political allegiances for the individual peasant in rural Poland. Although there is no denial of some historical similarities, certain differences, on the other hand, have been overlooked and the preceding quotation from W. I. Thomas and Florian Znaniecki's classic sociological work, *The Polish Peasant in Europe and America* (1927, Vol. II, p. 1440) suggests that the history and the role of the Church in Poland, in its bearing on the individual Catholic, may not have been as parallel to that in Ireland and Quebec as commonly thought.[17]

In terms of the concept of societal competition, cultural and religious differences were not as graphic in Poland as they were in Ireland and Quebec for several reasons. First, there was more diffuse heterogeneity within Poland, as a result of the many competing national and religious groups within constantly shifting and arbitrarily drawn boundary lines. Alicja Iwanska (1955, p. 189) cites figures that put the Catholic proportion of the Polish territory between World Wars I and II as approximately 65 per cent of the total. The remaining 35 per cent included Jews, the Eastern Orthodox, Protestants, and Eastern Rite Catholics, all representing different national origins. This kind of heterogeneity blurred the focus of religion and nationality that emerged with so much intensity in overwhelmingly Catholic Ireland and Quebec.

A second point might be made of the fact that Poland was geographically in confrontation with not one major power but two, flanking her on both sides; in the east there was Orthodox Russia, and in the west there was Protestant Prussia. Both situations, it has been argued, served to sharpen the consciousness of Polish national identity with the Catholic Church (Kolarz, 1946, p. 103). But at the same time, this dual confrontation became a thorn in the side of political compromise. Accommodation with one power at the expense of the other continually created problems not only for the Church but for the cause of Polish nationalism as well (Baron, 1960).

Complicating matters even more, Prussia had her own Catholic minority, and Poland of course had her different religious groups. All of these factors did not lead to any measure of unqualified or predictable support by the Vatican, or create the kind of symbolic competition that Catholic Ireland or Catholic Quebec experienced with the Protestant English. In both of these cases, the English were the only major problems perceived by the Catholics of Quebec and Ireland, and the energies of religious and national movement were all the more easily channeled in the one direction.

Within Poland too, the Church did not enjoy the same kind of secular support that it did in Ireland and Quebec. Its appreciation and backing by the peasants were largely limited to religious affairs. "Polish peasants were never very clear about how to define the role of their priest. They felt uncomfortable about the two overlapping roles of the parish priest, his secular role as the representative of the parish, and his religious role as the representative of God. The memoirs of Polish peasants of the interwar period reveal great bitterness toward their village priests" (Iwanska, 1955, p. 196).

It might be easily argued that memoir-writing is an avocation more often associated with the class of intellectuals than with the peasants, and that the foregoing quotation from Iwanska appears somewhat biased. But even at the level of the intellectuals and the educated classes, the differences with the view of the Church in Quebec and Ireland are apparent here.

One of the reasons for this disparity is the role the Church adopted within Poland toward the forces of social change. Thomas and Znaniecki

(1927, Vol. II, p. 1368) write of the breakdown of the peasant community and the lack of any vehicle for the reincorporation of Poles into a viable national community:

Religion and the church organization might have been, indeed, powerful means of unifying the peasant primary groups; but they could not be used, partly because of the unwillingness of the central Catholic Church authorities to let the Polish clergy commit itself in national and social struggles, partly because of the suspicion with which the Russian and Prussian governments looked upon the activities of the Polish clergy, partly also because of the undemocratic character of the church hierarchy.

In Poland, very few priests were found among the peasant leaders (Thomas and Znaniecki, 1927, Vol. II, p. 1310). The Church and its representatives were based on the existing social order, and they thwarted the drives toward change, especially in the field of popular education (Thomas and Znaniecki, 1927, Vol. II, p. 1298). Having little leadership among the clergy in secular affairs, the Polish Catholics did not identify their Church (in distinction to their religion) with a national identity to the degree evident among the Irish and the French-Canadians. The nature of societal competition was not as clearly expressive to the Poles, in terms of religion and ethnic conflict, as it was to these other two nationalities.

Parish organization itself appears to have been the salient basis of the traditional way of life in Poland, but there was a strong separation in the peasant's view of the role of the Church and the role of society. They did not merge in traditional Poland. Harold Finestone (1963, Chap. IV) compares the value systems and peasant communities of rural Poland and Southern Italy and finds that the Church has a greater integrative function in Poland than in Italy. In terms of societal competition, the integrative function of the Church and society finds still more expression in the history of Ireland and Quebec.

THE GERMAN CATHOLICS

Religiously the complexion of Germany was determined by the rulers of the several states. By the principle of *cuius regio, eius religio* every prince decided which form of Christianity would prevail in his domains. Some states were Catholic, some Lutheran, and some Reformed. Throughout the nineteenth century each state had its established church and sought to control ecclesiastical affairs within its borders. These *Landeskirchen* persisted into the twentieth century. In the empire Roman Catholics were a minority. At the close of the century they constituted about 36 per cent of the population. The North was fairly solidly Protestant. The Catholic Church was strongest in the South.

KENNETH SCOTT LATOURETTE (1958–1962)

The sixth and last group to be discussed are the Catholics of Germany. Although considered in the United States as among the most active supporters of the Catholic Church, the German Catholics share a kind of intermediacy with the Poles, in terms of the level of religious involvement.

The nature of cultural and religious competition in Germany has been a mixed phenomenon, as the foregoing quotation (Latourette, 1958–1962, Vol. I, p. 434) suggests. On the one hand, religious affiliation tended to predominate by region within the country. On the other hand, religious groups competed socially as a consequence of the political unification of the late nineteenth century, despite the fact that in all cases the groups are German.[18]

As Fogarty points out, and as cited at the beginning of this chapter, religious observance tends to be higher only in those areas of the country that are close to the frontiers of actual cultural competition. From the societal point of view, Catholicism in Germany is one of several religious affiliations. And from the regional or subsocietal position, Catholicism in Germany is either a majority or minority religion. This poses an important qualification to the overall societal pluralism.

For comparative purposes, societal competition in Germany or with cultural systems outside of Germany has been relevant to German history, but not nearly as exclusively as the conflicts between the Catholics of Quebec and Protestant Canada, or the struggles of Catholic Ireland with Anglican England. The presence of such competition is best illustrated by the *Kulturkampf* which Bismarck's Prussia waged with German Catholicism. The conflict between the Church and the forces for nationalist unification of Germany under the leadership of Protestant Prussia led in itself to the emigration of many German Catholics to the United States, for the expressed purpose of greater freedom in religious observance (Barry, 1953). Latourette (1958–1962, Vol. I, p. 292) associates this religious competition with the high involvement of German Catholics in the Church: "The effort to defeat Bismarck drew German Roman Catholics together and strengthened their loyalty to the Pope and their church."

On the other hand, much of the *Kulturkampf* varied by region, and the efforts of Bismarck to achieve national unity took advantage of regional differences. Accommodations were made with religious distinctions, and national interests seemed to prevail over sectional ones. The conflicts that were endemic between cultures and religions in Ireland and Quebec were not really sustained over time or pitched to the same degree of intensity in Germany.

With regard to religiocommunal organization, German Catholicism achieved considerable development. According to Latourette (1958–1962, Vol. I), Roman Catholicism in Germany attained a kind of national solidarity in sharp contrast to the divided Catholicism of France or the indifferent Catholicism of Italy. The solidarity was helped along by the conflicts with statism, but German Catholicism was popularly based on numerous associations organized early in the. nineteenth century. Associations with various institutional interests—the Centre Party, the Federation of Christian Trade Unions, the religious groups such as the Society of St. Boniface, and the populistic *Volkverein* and *Gesellenverein*—all contributed to the growth and involvement of German Catholics in their religion.

The twentieth century witnessed still more development. Organizational participation grew during the Weimar Republic. The most well-known Catholic associations were those of the trade unions and employers' groups for lay activity. But there were also "societies of mothers, of rural laborers, of store clerks, of school teachers, of waiters in hotels and restaurants, and to aid discharged prisoners." Latourette (1958–1962, Vol. IV, p. 185) documents the extent of activity within the Church at all levels of society. The rise of Nazism brought about the dissolution of most of these Catholic organizations, but involvement within the religion continued with a concentration of activity in the life of the parish.

German Catholicism appears to have been as well developed as the religion of Ireland and Quebec, especially in terms of parish communities and religious associations. But it is decidely communal in its cast. Largely because of regionalism, German Catholicism lacked the nationalist overtones that colored the religion of the Irish and the French-Canadians.

A SUMMARY AND OVERVIEW

Comparative data on specific developments in the religious history of each of the areas described are not easily available. By way of summary, however, some comparison may be made from recent data on the number of parishes and clergies reported for the different dioceses and sees within the Catholic Church. Tables 36 and 37 offer the ratios of Catholic population to the number of parishes and the number of clerics, respectively. The latter figures refer to the total number of diocesan priests, clergies in religious orders (males only), and seminarians.[19]

Table 36. Ratios of Catholic Population to Number of Parishes, Selected Countries and Provinces: 1949, 1953, 1957, 1961

Country or Province	Parish Ratios[a] (Number of Catholics per Parish)			
	1949	1953	1957	1961
Quebec	2,168	2,225	2,326	2,421
Germany	2,173	2,179	2,206	2,245
Ireland	3,041	3,078	3,067	3,028
Poland	3,645	3,358	3,658	3,529
Sicily	3,744	3,757	3,640	3,499
Mexico	10,295	11,310	11,768	14,511
Puerto Rico	18,485	20,047	18,468	20,513

[a] Ratios are calculated, to nearest whole number, from estimates of Catholic population and numbers of parishes, presented by sees and dioceses of each country shown. See Appendix tables for raw data. (Source: *Annuario Pontificio*, 1949, 1953, 1957, 1961.)

For both Tables 36 and 37, the ratios are provided for four different years (arbitrarily chosen, every fourth year after the data first were available in published form) for each of the countries or provinces discussed. Table 36 presents parish ratios, or the number of Catholics per parish in the designated area. It is suggested that the fewer the numbers of Catholics per parish, the more elaborate the organization of the Church for the given area. This is an indication of parish development, which serves as a clue to the distance between the Church and the religious involvement of the individual Catholics.

Table 37. Ratios of Catholic Population to Number of Clerics, Selected Countries and Provinces: 1949, 1953, 1957, 1961

Country or Province	Cleric Ratios[a] (Number of Catholics per Cleric)			
	1949	1953	1957	1961
Quebec	417	425	436	437
Ireland	423	410	383	356
Sicily	816	849	965	953
Germany	862	844	872	879
Poland	1,666	1,494	1,311	1,307
Mexico	3,501	3,336	3,100	3,657
Puerto Rico	6,512	6,479	5,216	4,948

[a] Ratios are calculated, to nearest whole number, from estimates of Catholic population and numbers of clerics (defined as diocesan priests, members of religious orders, and unordained seminarians), reported by sees and dioceses of each country shown. See Appendix tables for raw data. (Source: *Annuario Pontificio*, 1949, 1953, 1957, 1961.)

The rank orders of these parish ratios for the four years presented in Table 36 are very close, and the ratios themselves do not change considerably from one column to the next. If there is any bias in the reporting of these data, it does not seem to be erratic. The rank orders correlate fairly well with the religious behavior documented for the Catholic Americans originating from these countries and with the state of Catholicity arising from the degree of societal competition and cultural conflict.

There is evidence of greater parish organization for Quebec, Germany, and Ireland. Poland and Sicily are next in order, and Mexico and Puerto Rico are the least developed. In view of the condition of Catholicity in Latin America, and the factors discussed earlier, it is not surprising to see these parish ratios for Mexico and Puerto Rico. The ratios for Sicily, however, are higher than one might expect in view of the lack of formal involvement in Southern Italy. This is probably explained by the presence of the Vatican in Rome and the existence of a formal religious structure throughout Italy which has developed despite generalized indifference.

Table 37 offers the ratios of Catholic population to clerics. Nationalities of the priests are not known, but it is assumed that with some exceptions among religious orders and the missionary groups in Mexico and Puerto Rico most of the clergy and seminarians are native to the areas shown. These ratios may illustrate the extent to which clerical development varies with the different Catholic regions.

For the four years of Table 37, the rank orders are again very close to each other, and the ratios are fairly constant for the years reported. Ireland and Quebec are the lands of priests; the prevalence of clergy among the Irish and the French-Canadians confirms the past histories of these peoples.

Sicily is relatively well endowed with clergymen, on a level similar to Germany. Again, as with the indications of parish development, the traditions of Southern Italy and Sicily have produced an indifference to the Church in spite of well-organized parish systems and the availability of priests.

For the remaining three areas—Poland, Mexico, and Puerto Rico—the proportions of population to religious functionaries yield ratios of well over 1000. The ratios for Poland may reflect the newer post-World War II relation of church and state under communism. But the ratios for Mexico and Puerto Rico again confirm the expectation that there is littler clerical assistance for the size of the Latin American Catholic populations.

The comparative analysis of the historical backgrounds of six Catholic ethnic groups in the United States has explored selective facets of the nature of religioethnic systems. The major goal has been an explanation of the religious involvement of these ethnic groups primarily in terms of a model of societal competition based on religious and cultural differences.

The highest involvement of the Irish and the French-Canadians in the Catholic Church is a function of the intense societal competition each of these groups experienced throughout history. Catholics in other countries, whose social systems were not subject to the conflicts brought about by different religiocultural traditions, did not emerge with the religioethnic identification and close association with the Church which characterize the Irish and French-Canadians. Correlating with this kind of societal competition is a fairly well-developed parish system and religious communal organization.

The intermediate involvement of the German and Polish Catholics is explained by the mixture of competition that marked their histories. Catholics in Germany and Poland were subject to qualified degrees of competition and conflict, not equal to the intense feelings in Quebec and Ireland. Modifying factors, such as regionalism in Germany and the inconsistent role of the Church on social, economic, and political problems in Poland, prevented the complete identification of ethnicity with religion, which was so pervasive in Ireland and Quebec.

The lowest involvement of the Italian and Spanish-speaking Catholics is related to the lack of any societal competition which would have fostered the relevance of religious observance and the Church for these people. The indifference of the Latin Catholics is further traced to the factor of church-state alliances and the identification of the Church with the established order and against the movements for nationalism, social justice, and change.

Further research into this problem of religion and ethnicity may examine in greater detail the relevance of competition between cultural differences and the extent of religiocommunal organization for religioethnic involvement. The question of identification, always presumed in this study, needs to be tested directly for its religious and ethnic components and for the relationship it may have to social behavior. Furthermore, the influence of American society and the experiences after emigration to the United States are known to have an effect on the religiocultural traditions brought with the immigrants. Generation in this country has variable influence on the religious behavior of Catholic ethnic groups. What effect does interethnic marriage have on traditional religioethnic systems? This question is considered in Chapter Seven.

NOTES

1. The relationship between religion and ethnicity is also taken up by Warner and Srole (1945, pp. 156–161), when they briefly discuss the idea that national minorities throughout history, such as the Jews,

Greeks, Armenians, and different Catholic groups, who are subject to degrees of political domination and conflict, develop their own nationalities around their religious base.

2. Yinger (1963) has identified a number of problems and ideas in this area, most of which have yet to be examined with sustained interest and scholarship.

3. This chapter is limited to the backgrounds of these six groups (considering the Mexicans and Puerto Ricans together as Spanish-speaking), as the largest single ethnic traditions among Catholic Americans. Further research may consider the shape of religioethnicity and differentiation among specific Eastern European and other Roman Catholic nationality backgrounds.

4. This distinction is made by Blauner (1969) in the context of black-white relations in the United States.

5. The review is presented in the following order of involvement within the Church, as evidenced in Chapter Five: highest, the Irish and the French-Canadians; lowest, the Southern Italians and the Spanish-speaking; intermediate, the German Catholics and the Polish Catholics.

6. This is not meant to imply that all relations between clergy and laymen were close, or that divisions along ideological lines did not emerge among the Churchmen themselves. See O'Faolain (1949) for a discussion of these aspects as well. See also Burns (1962).

7. On the complications in the relations between the movement for nationlism and the institutions of Church and State, see Larkin (1962). For a discussion of the personification of this problem in James Larkin, the Irish labor leader, see Larkin (1965).

8. The argument for religioethnic distinctiveness may be clearer than the precise nature of the Irish Church or Irish Catholicism. O'Dea (1956) has pointed out that religion and nationality came to dominate the Irishman's conception of his self, partly because Catholicism in Ireland seldom assumed the posture of defensiveness. Despite the occasional clashes between religion and nationalism, as illustrated by the problems of Parnell, the norm was more likely to be the militance of the local clergy in support of the peasantry. On the other hand, Larkin (1964, p. 481) argues that competition created a specific defensiveness: "A hostile English Government in the seventeenth century, a proselytizing Protestantism in the eighteenth century, and a revolutionary Nationalism in the nineteenth century all had put the Irish Church on the defensive. The result was that the Church in Ireland reacted negatively rather than positively to the ways of the world." The difference in interpreta-

tion here may be due to the confusion between national identification and the ideology of nationalism. The former may have been less threatening and more of an immediately gratifying asset than the latter.

9. The historical pattern itself was probably one of increasing religious involvement over time. After the Great Famine of 1846, ironically, religious and related economic activity increased. See Larkin (1967).

10. In a recent survey, considerable ethnic differences were found in perceptions of Canadian society among youth. See Johnstone, Willig, and Spina (1969).

11. Consequently, as Wade (1946, p. 135) indicates, anticlericalism in Quebec was never very prevalent: "In the past, because of the great services of the clergy to national survival and because of the fact that it is democratically recruited from the people, anti-clericalism was confined to isolated individuals among the elite, who quarreled with clerical influence in politics, clerical monopoly of education, or clerical dominance in extra-religious fields."

12. See Verga's *Little Novels of Sicily* (1953, pp. 197–198). Many other novels also illustrate this mood. See, for example, Ignazio Silone, *Bread and Wine* (1937) and Carlo Levi, *Christ Stopped at Eboli* (1947).

13. The movement toward nationalism and the relations between Church and State in Italy were of course complicated, and much of what appeared as anti-Catholicism was more essentially the sentiment of anticlericalism; distinctions between the two phenomena were easily blurred. For discussion of this problem, see Mack Smith (1959, pp. 89–94, 222–230).

14. Montegrano is the fictitiously named commune in Southern Italy which was the location for Banfield's (1958) study of the conditions of political and communal organization.

15. In contrast again to the Irish, few priests wanted to accompany Italian Catholics during emigration, and few wanted to serve in Italian parishes in the United States. According to Vecoli (1969, p. 235), this was due not as much to the desire of Italian clergy to remain in Italy as it was to outright hostility and disrespect.

16. Countries such as Venezuela, Paraguay, Costa Rica, and Ecuador have concentrations between 50 and 78 per cent of their Catholic clergy in their capital cities. In Uruguay and Cuba, the percentages are even higher. See Rama (1967).

17. The Polish National Catholic Church is a more fitting example of the fusion of religion and ethnicity then Polish Roman Catholicism is. The Polish National Catholic movement illustrates a schism which responded

to the religioethnic needs of a people. Such a movement, I suggest, is not as likely among Irish and French-Canadian Catholics because these two systems already provide sufficient religioethnic identity for the Irish and French-Canadians who are in conflict with their Protestant environments. See Scagnelli (1970).

18. Competition, in terms of the "adjustment of multiple loyalties," is discussed by Gleason (1968, pp. 144–171) for German Catholics and German Protestants in America.

19. The source for these data is the *Annuario Pontificio,* the Vatican Yearbook, for the years, 1949, 1953, 1957, and 1961. The problem of reliability is considerable; data are reported by the diocesan curias concerned and are not subject to any controls. Another important problem is the shifting boundaries within dioceses and general population movements. I made the effort to include the total population of the same sees and dioceses for each year shown. Estimates of Catholics include all who are baptized as Catholics and who are not apostatized. A third problem is the gross comparability between these recent years and the historical decades of emigration to the United States. Unfortunately, similar figures are not available for years prior to World War II. As a result I am leaning on the assumption that these figures represent some continuity and historical pattern, unless otherwise noted. See the Appendix tables for the raw data on which the ratios are based.

CHAPTER SEVEN

CHANGING RELIGIOETHNIC BEHAVIOR

Channelling informal interaction within a group deepens the distinctiveness of the group further by keeping alive and developing the endo-culture of the group. Informal interaction creates primary relations that are governed by specific values, norms and beliefs. Interaction within the group will therefore lead to the maintenance or revival of group customs. Interaction out of the group, on the other hand, will lead to either the adoption of foreign customs or to the creation of new neutral customs. Sometimes, as in the case of many ethnic groups in U.S.A. today, a group might have lost its original language and much of its original traditional culture, but moral relations between its members will still be guided by endo-cultural symbols.

ABNER COHEN (1969)

IN THE PRECEDING CHAPTERS, I have explored a neglected question in the study of ethnic religion: What does it mean to be Irish Catholic, or German Catholic, or Italian Catholic, particularly in terms of religious involvement? The characteristics of religious behavior are aspects of cultural traditions: the intense association of the Irish and the French-Canadians with the Church, the more moderate involvement of the Germans and Poles, and the relatively indifferent behavior of the Italians and the Spanish-speaking of Latin America in formal Catholicism.

These cultural traditions, however, would still be expected to show signs of change in the course of the American experience after immigration. "Becoming American does not mean dissolving all differences, losing identity, and melting into the general masses of the population. Catholics do not cease to be Catholic when they become Americans; they cease to be Irish, or German, or French, or Polish" (Fichter, 1960, p. 116). Given the alternative interpretations of Americanization—of "becoming American" in Fichter's phrase, marrying into another ethnic group, becoming socially mobile, or having a background in the United States of three or more generations—what does ceasing to be Polish or French-Canadian or Irish mean? What kinds of influence do these forces have on religioethnic behavior? What kinds of changes are taking place within Catholicism as the traditional cultural components of the past assimilate through marriage?

THE MOVE FROM ETHNIC ENDOGAMY TO EXOGAMY

In anthropological and sociological literature, the concepts of endogamy and exogamy refer to the marriage patterns of distinct groupings in society, based on such ascriptive dimensions as caste, race, tribe, or clan. George Murdock (1960, p. 18) defines exogamy as a "rule of marriage which forbids an individual to take a spouse from within the local, kin, or status group to which he himself belongs." Conversely, endogamy is the "rule which requires him to marry within his own group."[1]

The distinctions inherent in these terms are important. The precise meaning of endogamy and exogamy lies in the fact that they are rules or institutionalized norms, prevalent among the traditional and ascriptive communities and societies studied by anthropologists. As diffuse and institutionalized norms, they can hardly be said to exist in the United States. The conspicuous exception is the history of codified laws forbidding marriages between the races in the Southern states and the noninstitutionalized but widespread norms against interracial marriage in most other parts of the United States.

The less precise, but nevertheless still informative use of these two terms as expressions of group marriage patterns in American society suggests preferential mating rather than that which is prescriptive. As noted in Chapter Two and Three, I was not able to explore the degree of pressure that different Catholic ethnic groups exert on the marriage choices of their members, and so the extent of prescription, if any, remains unknown. Endogamous marriage, as described and analyzed in this study, indicates at most only the individual's preference.

In the context of religioethnic change, however, the terms endogamy and exogamy are particularly useful because of their functional association with a given group's prevailing cultural and social system. Ralph Linton (1936, p. 204), for example, has suggested that endogamy helps to maintain the group's economic interests and social prerogatives. Kingsley Davis (1941) has spoken of the relationship of endogamy and the cultural compatibility of spouses. And Robert Merton (1941) has written that "endogamy ensures to a certain extent that the marriage contractants will have a rough similarity of cultural background inasmuch as they have been socialized in groups with similar culture."

Although these functional analyses are interpretations of endogamy in nominal caste or tribal societies, it can be assumed that the phenomena of endogamy and exogamy are even more widespread in their relevance and impact. Leslie White (1959, pp. 101–116) has argued to this point that many anthropologists have confused the idea of endogamy-exogamy, by writing about them as though they were distinct and discrete customs, either present or absent in any given society. This becomes somewhat misleading, White explains, because endogamy and exogamy are not cultural entities but rather social processes. As processes, they assume the forms of in-mating and out-mating and are applicable and relevant in all societies. The group which is the reference point may well vary, but both processes may be observed as simultaneous phenomena.

White (1959, p. 111) suggests that "the exogamous or endogamous features of social groupings on levels of cultural development considerably above the most primitive are merely further manifestations of these two processes." The scope of rules of endogamy and exogamy tends to be less extensive in literate than in preliterate societies, but the processes are nevertheless patterned and observable. This is true for the marriage patterns of Catholic ethnic groups in the data examined in preceding chapters.

The egalitarian themes of some societies urge the myths of free mating choices for all their members, but like the reality of any class- and status-stratified society, wide-open exogamy is not a universal phenomenon. Endogamy is expected to persist under certain social conditions or, at least operate simultaneously with exogamy, and White (1959, p. 114) explains some of its persistence:

> The purpose of endogamous rules and customs in advanced cultures is clear. Their objective is the same as in preliterate society: solidarity. And, of course, solidarity is not an end in itself. It is valued and striven for because solidarity means effective group effort, efficiency in the conduct of life, success in competition, perpetuation, and survival. Thus, for example, Jews favor endogamy because it promotes solidarity and effectiveness in group competition. Southern whites oppose marriage with Negroes because marriage would dissolve caste lines and thus remove the economic and political advantages they now enjoy over Negroes as a subject class.

White argues then that endogamy functions to promote group integrity in any social organization. The cultural behavioral style of the endogamous group is perpetuated and enhanced. In the heterogeneous organization of American society, certain processes of endogamy are particularly visible and effective in their maintenance of group solidarity. John Finley Scott (1965) has described the operation of college sorority practices as a means toward this end. Milton Gordon (1964) and Andrew Greeley (1971) have pointed out the networks of primary group relationships among upper-class Catholics in debutante parties, fashionable schools, and voluntary associations as operating in similar endogamous style. Perhaps the height of elaboration of the endogamy process in American society is suggested by the juncture of religion and nationality origin, as well as status, in the controlled mergers of the upper-class German Jewish "aristocracy" in New York during the past hundred years (Birmingham, 1966).

It is generally expected that endogamy will maintain the distinct values of the group and preserve the cultural forms peculiar to it. Exogamy, or intermarriage, on the other hand, may be expected to attenuate a group's traditional behavior. Murdock (1960, pp. 18, 184–259) has argued that exogamy leads to adjustments, that the phenomenon is associated with the evolution of social organization, and with cultural change as well. Marvin Harris (1959) has characterized exogamy as having a "leveling influence" on the culture and social order of subgroups in a pluralistic society. Intermarriage, according to Claude Lévi-Strauss (1969, pp. 42–51), tends to widen group interests and reduce both social inequalities and cultural distinctiveness.

Thus, under the general expectation that endogamy contributes to the maintenance of a group's traditional ethnic values and practices, and that exogamy operates as a vehicle of cultural change, what patterns result from marital changes within American Catholicism? I am proposing that the distinctive levels of religious involvement characterizing the different Catholic ethnic groups are subject to some pressures for change. Given the high association of religion and ethnicity for the Irish and the French-Canadians, exogamous marriage for these groups may produce a weakening of this tradition and bring about somewhat lower levels of religious involvement. Given the lower association of the Italian Catholics, exogamy with other groups within the Church may bring about higher levels of religious activity. Finally, because of the intermediate levels already characterizing the German and Polish Catholics, no consistent pattern in either direction is expected from marriage with other Catholic groups.[2]

CHANGES IN THE PARENTAL GENERATION

The specific analysis begins with an examination of religious behavioral change, as reported for the parents of the survey's respondents. Table 38 offers the percentage differences or changes in religious practice between the two types of marriages for the parental generation. Changes indicated by a minus sign point to a loss of involvement, and those of a plus sign denote increased association.[3]

Table 38. Percentage Change in Religious Behavior of Catholic Ethnic Groups, from Endogamous to Exogamous Marriage: Parental Generation

	Percentage Change in Religious Behavior (exogamous minus endogamous)					
Parental Religious Behavior[a]	Irish	French-Canadian	German	Polish	Italian	Total
Mass attendance: mother	−10	−12	−24	+5	0[b]	−3
Mass attendance: father	−8	−13	−6	−20	−4	+2
Communion: mother	−10	−26	−10	+15	−36[b]	−2
Communion: father	−4	−9	+1	+1	−4	+6
Catholic elementary school	−3	−15	+5	−11	+38	+12
Catholic high school	+2	−13	+5	+12	+13	+12

[a] Mass attendance percentage change refers to those going to Mass once a week or more; Communion refers to those receiving Communion once a month or more; Catholic schooling refers to those parents sending their children (the respondents) to available Catholic elementary or high schools.
[b] Percentage difference is based on an inadequate case base.

Consider first the two top rows of Table 38. There is some consistent change in attendance at Mass for both sexes of the Irish and the French-Canadians; both mothers and fathers of exogamous marriages are less dutiful in attendance at Mass than the Irish and French-Canadians of ethnically homogeneous marriages. The difference is at least 8 percentage points.

For the German Catholics, the mothers experience a decline in churchgoing with intermarriage, but the fathers do not. Among the Polish Catholics, the change with exogamy is the reverse; it is the fathers who fall away somewhat in church attendance. For the Italians, there is no apparent change for either sex, although the number of cases of exogamous Italian mothers is too small for any meaningful calculation.

The second two rows of Table 38 examine another measure of religious behavior among Catholics, the frequency with which Communion is received. Again, the endogamous Irish and French-Canadians are traditionally the most active in this aspect of church involvement, and both experience a decline with interethnic marriage. The only exception to this is for Irish fathers, who show virtually no difference. The behavior of the other three groups—the Germans, the Poles, and the Italians—is no more patterned on this measure of religious association than it was on Mass attendance.

Going to receive monthly Communion and attendance at weekly Mass are two distinct measures of religious formality, both serving as dimensions of church-going. Another kind of involvement lies in the support of the parochial school system, and exogamous marriage may have some influence on traditional styles of ethnic support. The last two rows of Table 38 reflect the changes between marriage types in this parental generation in sending children to Catholic schools. Controlling for the availability of parochial schools in the vicinity where each respondent was raised, the extent of change is noted.

Unlike their behavior in church attendance, the Irish parents clearly show no difference in their support of the Catholic school system; whether with Irish spouses or with other ethnic spouses, they remain among the most active supporters of the parochial schools. The French-Canadians, however, do decline. The exogamous French-Canadians are less likely to send their children to either Catholic elementary (by 15 percentage points) or Catholic high (by 13 points) schools.

The Germans show very little gain for both levels of the school system. The exogamous Polish Catholics are inconsistent, becoming less supportive of the elementary schools but more associated with the high schools. The only ethnic group to show considerable increase in parochial school support are Italians who leave their ethnic background and marry non-Italian Catholics. This is particularly true at the elementary school level.

In all of Table 38, the only *consistent* pattern is evidenced for the French-Canadians. There is an overall decline in formal association when this group moves from ethnic endogamy to exogamy. The Irish show signs of decline, but only incompletely. The German and Polish groups show mixed behavior as they become exogamous. And the expected rise of religious association for exogamous Italians is confirmed only by the gain in parental support of the respondents' attendance at Catholic parochial schools. Except for the loss of involvement for the exogamous French-Canadians, then, there is no other consistent pattern of religious change at this level, the parental generation. Of more considerable usefulness is a direct examination of the contemporary behavior of the Catholic respondents themselves, together with relevant social and religious control factors.

ETHNIC MARRIAGE AND CHURCH ATTENDANCE

Under the continuing assumption that religious and cultural behavior is maintained by the practice of group endogamy, what kinds of change in religious practice, if any, are associated with ethnic exogamy? As with Table 38 for the parental generation, Table 39 offers the percentage differences in Mass attendance for the endogamous and exogamous marriages of the respondents themselves. Declining involvement is measured by a minus sign, and increased association is indicated by a plus sign.

In Table 39, the percentage change in religious behavior for all Catholic Americans as they move from ethnic endogamy to exogamy (i.e., the *total* figures in the sixth column) is negligible. The findings for specific ethnic behavior, however, are different.

Since women are more likely than men to be church-goers, as noted in previous chapters, it would be of some value to see if exogamy has any influence on their religious involvement. The percentage differences in the first two rows of Table 39 suggest that this is the case. The Irish of both sexes show the same pattern: decline in church attendance. The French-Canadian females show no difference, but the males of this ethnic group display considerable loss of involvement once they choose wives from some other ethnic background.

Also in the first two rows of Table 39, the German and Polish Catholics of both sexes reveal no difference by type of marriage. As for the Italians, the women are more likely to attend weekly Mass if they have married outside of their group, but there is no comparable difference for the men. The fact of ethnic exogamy apparently is influential enough to affect the traditional behavior of Irish and Italian women (in their different ways) as well as have a bearing on Irish and French-Canadian men.

Table 39.   Percentage Change in Mass Attendance of Catholic Ethnic Groups, from Endogamous to Exogamous Marriage: Respondent's Generation

Respondent's Mass Attendance and Control Factors[a]	Percentage Change in Mass Attendance (exogamous minus endogamous)					
	Irish	French-Canadian	German	Polish	Italian	Total
Women	−11	+1	−5	+1	+11	+1
Men	−18	−26	+2	−4	−3	0
Newer generations	−43	−26	0	−8	+2	−2
Older generations	−13	−5	+2	+13	+11	−3
Lower education	−32	−37	−15	−8	+5	−5
Higher education	−11	+3	+3	+5	0	−1
Low parent religiousness	−30	−5	−2	+4	+6	+6
High parent religiousness	−7	−8	+1	−1	−2	−3
Low spouse religiousness	−60	−15	−20	0	−1	−5
High spouse religiousness	−1	+1	−2	−3	+6	+1
Prior Catholic schooling	−10	−16	−1	−1	+20	−4
Prior public schooling	−22[b]	−23[b]	+5[b]	−12[b]	+6	+10

[a] Mass attendance percentage change refers to those going to Mass once a week or more. Control factors are divided as follows: newer generations are first (the immigrants) and second (children of immigrants), and older generations are third (grandchildren of immigrants) and all later generations; lower education are those with some high school or less, and higher education are high school graduates or more; high parent religiousness, where both parents attended Mass once a week or more and both were weekly communicants, and low parent religiousness is anything less frequent than this; high spouse religiousness is spouse's weekly church attendance or more, and low spouse religiousness is anything less frequent than this; prior Catholic schooling, where respondent had some or all Catholic schooling, and prior public schooling, where respondent had only public schooling.
[b] Percentage difference is based on an inadequate case base.

Thus far, the phenomenon of decline in church and school involvement among the exogamous Irish and French-Canadians, although not entirely consistent, appears to be a fact more often than not. This loss of involvement, however, may be a function of generational residence in the United States, rather than a weakening of the ethnic factor through exogamy. The decline that does occur may be due to the fact (noted in earlier chapters) that exogamy is linked to those generations further removed from immigration, and the fact that Irish and French-Canadian levels of religious association tend to diminish somewhat among these very same third or later generations, as seen in Chapter Five. The following question then develops: What happens to the religious behavior of the first- and second-generation Irish and French-Canadians when they become exogamous? If the force of ethnicity *is* relevant among the immigrants and their children, then it would be reasonable to expect signs of such relevance with ethnic exogamy.

The third and fourth rows of Table 39 examine this question by pointing out the persistence of decline for the exogamous Irish and French-Canadians. Indeed, it is among the more recent immigrants that the change is greater. For the first- and second-generation Catholics, those Irish and French-Canadians who have left their nationality groups and have chosen spouses from other Catholic ethnic backgrounds are now among the *least* likely to be faithful to the requisite of weekly Mass attendance. For the Irish and the French-Canadians, ethnicity is bound up with religion, and the act of ethnic marriage is as important for religious behavior as the background of religious influence in the home is for maintaining ethnic attachments (cf. the section on ethnicity as a religiocultural force, in the discussion of the antecedents of ethnic marriage, Chapter Four).

For German and Polish Catholics, there is either no difference between types of marriages or there is a mixed phenomenon. With Italians, there is no change among the newer generations; the indifference pattern persists. Among older generation Italians, however, there is a sign of increased church attendance with interethnic marriage. The alleged acculturation of Italian Catholics to the "Irish norm" of religious behavior in the United States (discussed in Chapter Five) depends not so much on generation background alone then (Russo, 1968, 1970), but rather on the combined influence of generation and ethnic exogamy.

The general association of church-going and generation in the United States is connected with the Americanization of the immigrants and the socioeconomic status achieved. As one measure of social class, educational attainment is examined in the fifth and sixth rows of Table 39. The total figures in the last column of the table again show no difference in church attendance by kind of marriage, but they obviously mask the ethnic factor within Catholicism.

Among the better educated, type of marriage makes little difference for frequencies of Mass attendance, except for the Irish; there is some loss in this form of religious practice for the exogamous Irish. It is among those who never completed high school, however, that the ethnic attachments of marriage have more influence. The effect is most sharply felt among the Irish and the French-Canadians, as before, because of the close relationship of religion and ethnicity in these two traditions; the less educated Irish drop 32 percentage points in weekly Mass attendance when they marry non-Irish Catholics, and the comparable figure for the French-Canadians is even larger, 37 points.

In this connection, Andrew Greeley and Peter Rossi (1966) offer a number of relevant facts, as noted in Chapter Four. In their study, it was

pointed out, Catholics with higher levels of formal education tended to receive this schooling in the parochial school system, and both extent and type
of education contribute to increased religious observance. Since the Irish and
the French-Canadians are among the most active supporters of the Catholic
schools, those among them who received limited education in the public
schools are for purposes of this analysis deviant, and probably less likely to
be frequent church-goers. In this case, it is apparently *ethnic marriage* that is
responsible for their maintaining the ethnic culture; for choosing spouses
from other nationality backgrounds, as the fifth row of Table 39 shows,
makes them the *least* likely of all ethnic groups to continue tradition.

In addition to the factors of the social structure, some clarification of
those findings of the Irish and French-Canadians may be introduced by
looking into the relevance of specific religious influences. It is reasonable to
expect that the Irish and the French-Canadians who do leave their ethnic
backgrounds for marriage purposes do so because they are disposed to for
reasons of an atypical background. In other words, the exogamous Irish and
French-Canadians may be those whose parental homes had less religious influence to begin with, or those whose exogamous spouses were and are not as
inclined to attend weekly church services. The data of this survey do not
allow for an examination of the respondent's own disposition toward religion during the years before his marriage, but the influence of parents and
spouse can be ascertained. These factors can further specify the strength of
the ethnic factor itself.

The seventh and eighth rows of Table 39 control for the degree of
parental religious involvement, based on an index of parental practices; high
involvement indicates that both parents attended Mass as frequently as once
a week, and one or both were weekly communicants, while low involvement
measures any less frequent religious expression (Greeley and Rossi, 1966, p.
44). Among the Irish from homes with less religious influence, the fact of
ethnic exogamy reduces Mass attendance by 30 percentage points. For the
French-Canadians, as for the other groups shown in the table, exogamy does
not make much difference. With Irish Catholics, however, the importance
of ethnicity persists.

The influence of the spouse, as suggested in earlier chapters, would
seem considerable, and a direct examination of this factor in the ninth and
tenth rows of Table 39 confirms the expectation. Despite the influence of
the spouse as a strong factor in church-going, there is nevertheless notable
change for both the Irish and the French-Canadians who have married out
of their own backgrounds and whose spouses are less likely to be regular
church-goers.

The endogamous Irish with less involved spouses tend to remain high on
church attendance. When their spouses are not Irish, the proportion drops by

an overwhelming 60 percentage points. Similarly, if less spectacularly, there is a 15-point decline for the exogamous French-Canadians with less involved spouses. Thus the previous findings are not solely due to the idea that Irish and French-Canadian Catholics who marry into other backgrounds are more likely to be marrying Catholics who are less associated with the Church, or because of their indifference to religion. The fact of ethnic marriage itself is clearly important.

The last two rows of Table 39 control for the type of schooling the respondent himself received. It has already been noted that parochial schooling leads to more regularity in the exercise of religious duties. The question now is whether the type of ethnic marriage makes any further difference for religious behavior. The findings for the Irish, the French-Canadians, and the Italians suggest that it does. Among respondents with some or all of their education in the Catholic schools, the endogamous Irish and French-Canadians are again more likely to attend weekly Mass than are their exogamous counterparts. The reverse is true for the Italians; their association with the Church rises with exogamy *and* a background of parochial school education.

ETHNIC MARRIAGE AND CATHOLIC SCHOOL SUPPORT

Attendance at Mass is only one aspect of involvement in formal religion for Catholic Americans. Another measure may be obtained by looking at patterns of support for the parochial school system. Table 40 provides these data in exactly the same way that Table 39 offered them for church attendance. All figures in Table 40 control for the availability of Catholic schools in the neighborhoods where the respondents themselves are living and where these Catholics have sent their children for schooling.

Does the type of ethnic marriage have any influence in decisions for sending children to the Catholic school system? The point is clear again that the Irish and French-Canadian Catholics are less likely to support the religious schools when they leave their own ethnic backgrounds and marry out. The first row of Table 40 shows a decline of 11 and 14 points, respectively, for these two groups, and no comparable pattern for either the total sample of all Catholics or any other specific group. The German and Polish Catholics show mixed behavior, and unlike the pattern of increased school support for exogamous Italian parents, the Italian respondents themselves show no change in their parochial school involvement with exogamous marriage.

For the remaining rows of Table 40, with consideration of the different control factors discussed in Table 39, and with the qualification of inadequate

Table 40.   Percentage Change in Parochial School Support by Catholic Ethnic Groups, from Endogamous to Exogamous Marriage: Respondent's Generation

| Respondent's School Support and Control Factors[a] | Percentage Change in Catholic School Support (exogamous minus endogamous) | | | | | |
	Irish	French-Canadian	German	Polish	Italian	Total
Catholic school support	−11	−14	+10	−6	−4	+4
Newer generations	+5	−22[b]	+20[b]	−12	−3	+5
Older generations	−19	−22	+15	+22	−33[b]	−7
Lower education	−9	−32[b]	+17	+3	+17	+7
Higher education	−11	−8	+5	−17	−21	−3
Low parent religiousness	−10	−47[b]	+33[b]	−4	+3	+9
High parent religiousness	−12	+2	+7	−4	−15	0
Low spouse religiousness	+1[b]	0[b]	+17[b]	−17[b]	+11	+11
High spouse religiousness	−11	−14	+8	−4	−14	−1
Prior Catholic schooling	−10	−13	−1	−2	−21	−5
Prior public schooling	−13[b]	−17[b]	+55[b]	−34[b]	−14	−1

[a] Percentage change in Catholic school support refers to those sending their children to locally available parochial schools. Control factors are identical to those used in Table 39 and are explained in a footnote to that table.
[b] Percentage difference is based on an inadequate case base.

numbers of cases in some instances, the Irish and the French-Canadians show the persisting phenomenon of decline in parochial school support with ethnic exogamy. The Germans show consistent gain on this measure, but they do not in Table 39 with data on church attendance. The Polish and Italian Catholics still reveal no patterned behavior.

Consider the examples of the Irish and French-Canadians more closely. Even among the older (third or later) generations, the more educated, those with spouses who are regular church-goers, and, above all, those with prior Catholic schooling themselves, there is some decline in involvement with the parochial school system for the exogamous Irish and French-Canadians. The Irish and French-Canadians who married out of their ethnic backgrounds are less supportive of Catholic schools, despite the fact that they themselves had attended such schools or have characteristics which (as shown in preceding chapters) usually dispose one toward similar or increased association with the formal religion.

It is evident here that the Irish and French-Canadian Catholics do fall away from the high level of association with the Church which has long been traditional for these two groups. The falling away, of course, is not at all a sign of apostacy, but merely a modification of the Irish and French-Canadian religioethnic systems taking place through the marital assimilation of Catholic Americans.

SUMMARY

The mechanism of endogamy does maintain the group's cultural style (and, conversely, exogamy does attenuate or modify that culture) *if*, as in the cases of the Irish and the French-Canadians, the religious practice is integrated with the distinctive culture or ethnicity. The role of ethnicity within religion and the Catholic Church is all the more striking for the traditions of the Irish and the French-Canadians essentially because of the absence of any patterned change when other groups intermarry. These groups—the Germans, the Poles, and the Italians—for whom involvement in religious practice has been characteristically less of a function of nationality, or even one of traditional indifference to the meaning of nationality, show no consistent changes with ethnic exogamy. The German and Polish religioethnic styles are neither the most involved with the Church nor the least involved, and, consequently, the act of ethnic marriage would not necessarily influence any change in any particular direction. The Italian traditions in formal Catholicism, grounded in indifference for so long a period of time, persist with ethnic intermarriage. These show some signs of increased association only under the combined conditions of exogamy *and* structural forces such as accumulated generational experience in America. Furthermore, one could argue that if any groups were to show patterned change, one would expect it from precisely those groups for whom the meanings of ethnicity and religion are so historically integrated.

It is clear at this point in the research that the fact of ethnicity itself has implications for the area of religious behavior. The fusion of religion and nationality in the histories of Ireland and Quebec was such that changes in ethnic attachments, as examined here through marriage choice, have relevance for changes in religious attachments. Where historical developments for other Catholic backgrounds did not foster the acute interpenetration of religion with a national feeling, the specific relevance probed here did not emerge.

NOTES

1. Sociologists have used the terms of endogamy and exogamy interchangeably with other expressions; endogamy has been used synonomously with

"in-marriage" and "in-group marriage," and exogamy is often equated with "intermarriage," "out-group marriage," or "mixed marriage."

2. The most direct test of this idea would be a comparison of the religious behavior of individual Catholic Americans with spouses of the same and of differing ethnicity. This is the procedure used in this chapter. Because of the very impossible dispositions to be less involved in religion to begin with, as influences prior to the act of marriage, controls for the religious background of the parental home, the fact of public or parochial schooling for the respondent, and the extent of religious involvement of the spouse will all be employed. The analysis focuses on five selected groups, all of whom afford sufficient numbers of both endogamous and exogamous cases: the Irish, French-Canadians, Germans, Poles, and Italians. The Spanish-speaking must be omitted from this specific analysis because of their fewer exogamous respondents. Another important omission is the detailed examination of exogamous pairs. As noted in Chapter Three, the exogamous choices of specific ethnic Catholics are too few to allow for a systematic analysis of behavior resulting from, say, Irish-Italian or German-Polish marriages. Findings presented in this chapter will refer only to the fact of exogamy, and particular ethnic combinations must await future research.

3. Further information on the detailed tables which are summarized in Table 38, and in Tables 39 and 40 on subsequent pages of this chapter, may be found in Abramson (1969, pp. 191–220; 1971).

Part Four

The Ethnic Factor in American Life

CHAPTER EIGHT

THE QUESTION OF ETHNIC PLURALISM

America was meant to be everything. . . . There are many soils and many climates included within the boundary line of the United States; many *countries*; and one rule cannot be laid down for all.

HARRIET MARTINEAU (1837)

We are the Romans of the modern world—the great assimilating people.

OLIVER WENDELL HOLMES (1858)

Settled by the people of all nations, all nations may claim her for their own. You can not spill a drop of American blood without spilling the blood of the whole world. . . . We are the heirs of all time, and with all nations we divide our inheritance. On this Western Hemisphere all tribes and people are forming into one federated whole.

HERMAN MELVILLE (1849)

"I'm Polish. . . . I don't know who's really American. There are guys I work with, they're Italian and Irish. They're different from me, even though we're all Catholics. You see what I mean? We're buddies on the job. We do the same work. We drink our coffee together and sit there eating lunch. But you leave and you go home and you're back with your own people. I don't just mean my family, no. It's more than your wife and kids; it's everything in your life."

ANONYMOUS (Coles and Erikson, 1971)

OF THE PARTICULAR SUBSTANTIVE MATTERS dealt with in this book, two general conclusions stand out. It is clear that ethnic diversity has not yet disappeared in America, despite the apparent standarization of the country in more overt, visible, superficial forms, and despite all the predictions over time that ethnicity is dead. As with the reports of Mark Twain's demise, the prophecies have been greatly exaggerated. It is also clear, furthermore, that as an explanation for subsequent changes in life styles of ethnic groups, the mere accumulation of generational residence in America does not suffice.

The persistence of ethnic values and traditional behavior as well as the extent of ethnic variation in patterns of change are challenges to a sociology of American society. We have yet to develop an understanding of the nature of change in a country that was shaped by the massive ethnic forces of voluntary and involuntary immigration, of slavery and bondage, and of exploitation and genocide. Our neglect of the meaning and influence of ethnicity stands out in marked contrast, say, to our more fully developed appreciation of the concept of social class. The reality of diversity—racial, religious, national origin, regional, and combinations of these—is still very much with us.

The three historic alternatives of cultural policy and prediction have not been adequate avenues of ethnic speculation (Gordon, 1964, pp. 84–159). One of the earliest expressions of the melting pot notion was provided by Jedidiah Morse (1789): "The time . . . is anticipated when the language, manners, customs, political and religious sentiments of the mixed mass of the people who inhabit the United States, shall have become so assimilated, as that all nominal distinctions shall be lost in the general and honourable name of Americans." But the melting pot, that process of amalgamation which would result in a new breed of man, unlike any particular ethnic stock and yet a fusion of all cultural backgrounds, that mythical transformation of behavior and character, as Nathan Glazer and Daniel Patrick Moynihan (1963) and more recently Michael Novak (1971) have pointed out, has not happened.

Ethnic conformity to Anglo-American models of thought and practice has not come to pass either, and this seems truer in the 1960s and 1970s than it has in some time. Conformity, of course, is a matter of degree, and it is obvious that some ethnic groups are closer to the cultural values and behav-

173

ioral styles of Anglo-Saxon Protestant America than others. It is also obvious that some Anglo-American values and institutions (such as the English language and the British legal system) attract more conformity and adherence than other characteristics of Anglo-America (such as the Protestant Ethic and the nuclear family), for a variety of reasons.

The expectations of overall conformity in the nineteenth century and the goals of the Americanization movement in the early twentieth century cannot be said to be fulfilled. "The tendency of things is to mould the whole into one people, whose leading characteristics are English, formed on American soil," one writer remarked in 1848.[1] Seventy years later, American society was even more heterogeneous, and national movements and collective efforts to induce conformity tried to match strides with the diversity of the population. The different stages and emphases of "Americanization" constituted, in Milton Gordon's (1964, pp. 98–99) words, "a consciously articulated movement to strip the immigrant of his native culture and attachments and make him over into an American along Anglo-Saxon lines." Yet even now, in the late twentieth century, ethnic variation manages to persist.

The third response to the existing diversity of American society was termed cultural pluralism, and its foremost exponent was the social philosopher Horace Kallen.[2] Cultural pluralism, as Kallen (1956) discusses it, and in contrast with the two preceding ideologies of American diversity, does come closest to the existing realities of ethnic heterogeneity in the United States, but it does not provide much of a sociological base for research and analysis. Kallen applauds the *value* of ethnic communality in a widely mixed America: as significant to the individual and the group to which he belongs on the basis of tradition, as significant to the consistent ideals of difference *and* equality which emerged in the ideological beginnings of America, and as significant to the nation as a whole which becomes all the richer as a result of the contributions of its ethnic parts (Gordon, 1964, pp. 144–147). Kallen wrote, as recently as 1956 (p. 98):

> This process is an orchestration of . . . diversities—regional, local, religious, ethnic, esthetic, industrial, sporting and political—each developing freely and characteristically in its own enclave, and somehow so intertwined with the others, as to suggest, even to symbolize, the dynamic of the whole. Each is a cultural reservoir whence flows its own singularity of expression to unite in the concrete intercultural total which is the culture of America.

From the sociological perspective, Kallen is overstating his argument for cultural pluralism, perhaps out of wishful thinking and the rhetoric of ideology. There is ethnic diversity to be sure, but American society is not certainly a pluralist federation of cultures in the sense of certain African and Caribbean societies (Kuper and Smith, 1969). There is marital assimilation, as preceding chapters in this book have shown for Catholic ethnic groups, but this is neither enough to warrant the conclusion that the melting pot has worked nor too little to prove that ethnic endogamy is the norm for all groups. There is some ethnic value change, but neither enough to indicate that Anglo-American life styles have come to be expected ways of life for all citizens nor too little to argue the existence of graphic forms of cultural and structural separation for American ethnic groups.

When we limit the perspective to race, and when we examine American society in its composition of different socially defined racial groups, based on physical characteristics, we observe that the United States has developed with different degrees of integration: the more integrated ethnic sectors of white America, and the less integrated ethnic sectors of nonwhite America. Integration and assimilation are relative phenomena in American society.

Although race is the most salient ethnic factor, it is still only one of the dimensions of the larger cultural and historical phenomenon of ethnicity.[3] The sociological problem then is ethnic variation in change as much as it is ethnic variability in culture. And it is the persisting diversity within *white* America which remains to be considered: the diversity that clings to the class system, religious involvement, marriage patterns, as well as the diversity of regionalism, politics, communities, and power. We will have a better understanding of racial diversity if we pay more attention to the broader phenomenon of ethnic diversity at large. If ethnic life persists within the white society, within Catholicism, within the urban environment and the rural sectors, across regions and several generations of experience in America, what might this tell us about the more visible and more dramatic racial differences that remain, again for both unsolicited malevolent reasons of racism and ethnocentrism and for voluntary supportive reasons of ethnic attachment and group identity?

ETHNIC PERSISTENCE AND CHANGE

To return to the specific analysis described in this book, I wish to make a number of particular points about the role of ethnicity in American life. In doing so, I will contrast the model of generational influence discussed in Chapter Five with the explicit model of societal competition offered in Chapter Six, in order to summarize specific ethnic changes in the American context.

Catholic ethnic groups brought to America their own distinctive styles of life, through the process of transplanting ethnic forms and interests. Each group's religious behavior, it has been argued, was shaped in part by the degree of societal competition experienced in the country of emigration. Thus a model was developed for explaining comparative similarities and differences with regard to formal religious involvement within a shared religion, by inquiring into the peculiarly ethnic sources of sociocultural behavior and religious diversity.

At the same time, the forces of generational change in the United States are presumed to be influencing the ethnic and religious behavior of the immigrants and their descendants. The "Americanization" process, as it has been called, has seldom been analyzed in any empirical sense, but the implications of higher social status, increased social mobility, more education, and a generalized loss of ethnic distinctiveness are often viewed as the ingredients of acculturation and, more broadly, the levels of assimilation. Milton Gordon's (1964, pp. 60–83) discussion of structural assimilation—the increasing frequency of the interaction of the ethnic minority with nonethnics in the society on the primary group level—subsumes the phenomenon of intermarriage or exogamy and specifies the meaning of assimilation.

On the basis of generational change alone, we might expect some modification of the religious behavior that has been characteristic of the ethnic group itself, if only because the accumulation of life experience in America would deemphasize the important and salient historical attachments of the group's past. The analysis in this book, however, specifies the influence of the factor of generational background not only in terms of persisting or changing ethnic solidarity (the fact of endogamy versus exogamy), but also in terms of the historical origins of religioethnic affiliation. This kind of specification allows us to examine the influence of the generational factor with a greater awareness of the kind of change taking place.

For the Irish and the French-Canadian Catholics, generational background in the United States does tend to modify the religious involvement which is historically traditional for these groups. But it is the factor of ethnic exogamy that specifies this downward direction, because out-group marriage would interrupt the cultural continuity and reinforcement a spouse of the same ethnicity would potentially provide. Both factors of generation and exogamy are especially relevant for the Irish and French-Canadians, it was argued, because of the historical backgrounds of these two groups. When they are removed from the societal and cultural competition of traditional Ireland and Quebec, and without the supports implicit in endogamous marriage, it is easier to understand the fact that Irish and French-Canadian religious involvement becomes more relaxed in American society. The factor of generation alone is not enough of an explanation of the changing religious behavior of the Irish and French-Canadian Catholics.

The same kind of patterned explanation does not hold for the German and Polish Catholics. Since ethnic exogamy does not introduce as sharp a discontinuity to their cultural pasts, which in themselves are more qualified fusions of religion and nationality, it may be argued that generation alone *is* sufficient to explain their changed religious involvement. The influence of American society has been to increase German and Polish Catholic involvement, and ethnic exogamy does not specify any degree or direction for such behavior. The increase over time of church attendance and support of the Catholic school system is probably due to the influence of American norms, in this case the traditional model of the visible Irish and the acculturation of German and Polish Catholics toward Irish norms within American Catholicism. More specific research on the role of ethnicity in German and Polish Catholic communities in the United States may contribute to our understanding of these changes.

For Italian Catholics, the logic of the argument developed here would suggest that both generation and exogamous influences would lead to increased religious involvement. It would seem reasonable to expect evidence of change, inasmuch as the force of generation in America and ethnic exogamy would contribute to a weakening of the pervasive cultural past of the Southern Italians. The data, however, suggest that generation itself has no influence on Italian religious behavior; indifferent levels of activity persist. Exogamy does specify some influence of increased church attendance, but the numbers of exogamous Italians themselves of third or later generations are too few in this study to permit any definite conclusions.

The explanation of the level of relative religious indifference among Italians of different generational backgrounds is traced to the persistence of Italian residential communities in the United States, most of which are endogamous and closely knit. When exogamy does take place among third and later generations, there seems to be some influence manifest in increasing church involvement. Further research on changing and persisting cultural behavior of the Italian Americans must consider the influence of ethnic exogamy as well as generational background.

The factor of generation itself, then, is not always sufficient to explain or point to any widespread pattern of religious change that would be universally characteristic of American ethnic groups. Will Herberg's (1955) thesis of changes in the religious association among the immigrants, their children, and the third generation is not sustained. The findings of Gerhard Lenski (1961) and others on consistent increases in church attendance by generational background for the undifferentiated Catholic population are not supported for those Catholic groups whose religious backgrounds are either fused with the meaning of nationality or distinctly separate from the ethos of nationality.

It is evident that a major reason for the lack of uniformity on the "three-generation hypothesis" is the fact that so little attention has been paid to the ethnic factor as a source of differentiation in American life. The assumption that ethnicity in the form of national origin is no longer a relevant factor is unfortunate. This complaint should not convey the idea that social change is any less prevalent, or that assimilation in its different manifestations is any less meaningful, in the course of American society. Rather, the assumption that ethnicity is irrelevant is unfortunate precisely because the assumption is misleading.

First, and most obviously, this orientation does not facilitate research in those regions of America and for those aspects of social behavior where the ethnic factor most visibly does persist, not as a kind of "apparent anachronism" (a term frequently offered by those who are rather impatient with the phenomenon), but in the newer form of interest groups as described by Glazer and Moynihan (1963). Variations by ethnic background emerge fairly regularly, consistently, and with real effects in studies of politics, family life, and, as documented in this book, religious involvement. The problem for sociology does not lie merely in describing the persistence of the ethnic factor but also in explaining it. And perhaps future research in the field of ethnicity and ethnic identity will offer explanations which are lacking at this point in time.

But even more important for the sociology of American society or any pluralistic community, ignoring ethnicity as a source of differentiation inhibits our understanding of the process of change. If, in the American past, the ethnic factor was indeed a most important source of heterogeneity, it is reasonable to expect ethnic variation in change itself, as subcultural forms interact with the wider structural currents of the larger society.

Much previous research has assumed that ethnic differentiation is acted upon by the homogenizing forces of mass society, and the influence is presumed to be both total and unilateral. The expectation is a standardization of behavior with a fairly uniform directional change, on an underlying basis of diversity. The trouble with this point of view is that it ignores history and the origins of differentiation. One of the more obvious problems arising from this position is the failure to discern the nature of the norm or model to which ethnic groups are assimilating, or around which ethnic behavior is being standardized. Vague descriptions of "core society" and "Anglo-conformity" are difficult to appreciate in studies of acculturation and social change in the United States. More extensive comparative analysis of the historical developments of society would facilitate contemporary investigation into the process of social change by clarifying the roots of diversity and specifying the different patterns of changing behavior and identification.

The assimilationist bias in American sociology and history has clouded the distinctiveness of ethnic experiences in the United States and has ignored the role of ethnic minorities in the American consciousness. This bias has contributed to a neglect not only of the meaning of ethnicity and subcultural identification but also of the varied changes involved in diversity and pluralism. If ethnic diversity remains a reality among white Catholic Americans, after several generations of life in the United States, and despite the movement of Catholic ethnic groups into higher socioeconomic status levels, then are we not obliged to reconsider the nature of ethnicity as a basis of pluralism in America?

ETHNIC DIVERSITY AND THE AMERICAN MOSAIC

A model of ethnic pluralism, in association with the distribution of class and status variables, will describe American society more realistically than it has been described thus far. An interpretation of the past in both ethnic and socioeconomic terms will undoubtedly provide a sounder basis for understanding the American experience and for dealing with the role of minority groups in the contemporary world. Group conflict and accommodation, and the issues of social, economic, and political power, are inevitably tied to ethnic differences in the United States, just as they are to the differences of social class. Ethnicity and class are the two major segmenting influences in American society.

In another context, a study of political socialization, David Easton and Jack Dennis (1969, p. 41) criticize the common assumption that stability requires the elimination of individual and group differences. "The tendency to interpret homogeneity as a condition of stability is perhaps linked with the almost instinctive dominance of the melting-pot concept of society in the United States. . . . The levelling of linguistic and religiocultural differences has hitherto been accepted almost without question as a preferred state of affairs." The authors propose an alternative conceptualization of American society as a multiethnic mosaic, in contrast to the cultural homogeneity so frequently assumed in social science research (p. 407):

> . . . the United States is and has been a multi-ethnic society, however unwilling it has been to conceptualize itself in these terms. For certain historical reasons, perhaps because the major minority group rose out of legal slavery and then has remained in social bondage for almost a century, American society has been able to deny the reality.

The racial crisis of the 1960s has vividly revealed that even though the prevalent white and Anglo-Saxon ideology has been built around melting-pot aspirations, and even though this has militated against alternative ways of conceptualizing the American social context, the United States has been unable to escape the strife and turbulence of many other multi-ethnic societies. American ideology has failed to constrain American reality. This may ultimately force the United States to alter its political self-image radically so that it may begin to reinterpret itself for what it really is, a society composed of several large and residentially concentrated ethnic groups—black, Puerto Rican, Mexican-American, American Indian, and others—in tense juxtaposition to the dominant white, English-speaking population.

There are several very important ideas explicit and implicit in these remarks. Foremost among them is the nature of American society as an ethnically mixed society, and the relationship of this fact to American thought. The reasons for the neglect of ethnic diversity, the explanations themselves, would provide enough material for an intriguing study in the sociology of knowledge.[4] Whatever the ideological and background factors, the problem today confronts us very directly in the way Americans view themselves and their country, and how they behave.

The existent diversity is evident enough to assure us that it is not ephemeral. Ethnicity in America may seem to wax and wane as a social and political issue, but there is obviously more to it than we presently understand. The ethnic factor for white Catholic Americans remains important, in conjunction with social class and region of the country, in marriage patterns and ethnic attachments, and in organizational and associational life such as religion, the institutional example studied in this book. Accordingly, ethnicity and class provide a macrosociological matrix for the perception of a society, not unlike John Porter's (1965) description of Canada. In this regard, Milton Gordon's (1964) notion of the "ethclass" becomes very relevant, not only at the behavioral level of the individual as Gordon discusses it, but also at the societal level of the interaction of groups.[5]

Ethnicity is more important at the lower status levels of the class system. It has greater influence, for example, among the lesser educated, the blue-collar occupations, the inner-city neighborhoods, and the poor. This is not to say that ethnicity is unimportant at the middle-class levels of America, but only that it is less visible because of the apparent uniformities of middle-class life styles.[6] Just how important ethnicity is in many different areas of social behavior, comparatively for specific ethnic backgrounds *and* for specific institutional life, remains to be tested.

Among the poor or the relatively poor, ethnicity stands out not only in the way the poor may subjectively identify themselves, but also in the way the rest of the society identifies *them*. Poverty may be unique in the United States (or in any other ethnically plural society), because the poor have something other than poverty with which to identify, and the rest of the society or region or community often has a referent for the poor which attaches to one particular ethnic group or another. Thus it has been and it still is the ever-shifting mosaic of ethnicity and class: the Southern black sharecroppers as the poor, the Mexican migrant workers as the poor, the Italian construction and railroad workers as the poor, the Jewish textile workers as the poor, the French-Canadian mill hands as the poor, the American Indians on the reservations as the poor (and less obviously, for their Anglo-Saxon Protestant antecedents, the Appalachian miners as the poor, the Swamp Yankees of New England as the poor, and the Okies of the Dust Bowl as the poor). Regardless of the actual distribution of resources, ethnicity intrudes into one's perception of subjective and objective status groups. Herman Melville's *Redburn* (1849) offers a very relevant insight into this phenomenon, when the author has his protagonist comment on the poverty in Liverpool (p. 202):

> In these haunts, beggary went on before me wherever I walked, and dogged me unceasingly at the heels. Poverty, poverty, poverty, in almost endless vistas: and want and woe staggered arm in arm along these miserable streets.
>
> And here, I must not omit one thing, that struck me at the time. It was the absence of negroes; who in the large towns in the "free states" of America, almost always form a considerable portion of the destitute. But in these streets, not a negro was to be seen. All were whites; and with the exception of the Irish were natives of the soil; even Englishmen; as much Englishmen, as the dukes in the House of Lords. This conveyed a strange feeling: and more than anything else, reminded me that I was not in my own land. For *there*, such a being as a native beggar is almost unknown; and to be a born American citizen seems a guarantee against pauperism.

It was amazing to Melville to comprehend that the poor in Liverpool were as English as the "dukes in the House of Lords." And to turn to the other side of this idea, it was startling to recall that the poor in America in the middle decades of the nineteenth century were something other than native-born whites. Of course, Melville was wrong in this view; there were substantial numbers of the poor who were indeed native-born whites, and large proportions of the American-born whites were poor, just as they are today. The important and curious aspect of this phenomenon, however, is what may be called the "definition of the situation." Poverty, to a dominant group, may be perceived as a problem adhering to minority groups of differing ethnicity, at least in terms of salient identificational purposes. Poverty is something that is characteristic of other groups, when there are other groups; this may be the sense of the phenomenon as felt by the majority group in an ethnically plural society. Objectively, many people of many backgrounds may be poor, but subjectively, it is easier to define oneself (even when indeed poor) as "better off" than that other group on the other side of town, or even next door.

The relationship between ethnicity and class is considerably involved and deserves a great deal more attention than it has received thus far, whether in the larger view, the macrosociological perception of America as a multiethnic mosaic, or on the more microsociological level of individual ethclass relations. It is beyond the scope of this concluding chapter to go into greater detail or speculation on the nature of this relationship; the intention has been only to set down some exploratory thoughts.

An additional issue, following from the Easton and Dennis quotation cited earlier, refers to the fact that "the United States has been unable to escape the strife and turbulence of many other multi-ethnic societies." The Black Movement of the 1960s and 1970s has urged upon us a reassessment of American society. There has been a history of violence and ethnic cleavage in the American past, as well as history of social mobility and progressive change.[7] The ethnic and economic interests in Black Power among Afro-Americans in the United States and the struggles of Chicanos in agriculture in the Western states follow the tradition of the Molly Maguires among the Irish coal workers in Eastern Pennsylvania, the conflicts of Italian laborers in New Orleans and the railroad towns of Colorado, or the efforts of the Chinese to ward off massacres and lynchings in the Far West. The tradition is one that combines ethnicity and economic necessity, and one that usually combines elements of powerlessness with ethnic differences.

Any conception of America and the American past in terms of ethnic diversity and the division of labor and resources will have to go beyond the assimilationist bias that all ethnic minorities desire to conform to dominant styles of behavior, beyond the consensual model of American pluralism which acknowledges the existence of ethnic groups but deemphasizes the conflict involved in ethnic accommodation, and beyond the assumption that social and political organization must necessarily achieve stability and equilibrium through ethnic homogeneity and cultural consensus.

The ethnic diversity among Catholic Americans—throughout the social structure, for different regions of the United States, across generational lines, in patterns of endogamy and exogamy, and in traditional styles of religious involvement—illustrates the diversity that characterizes America. The persistence of some forms of ethnicity over time is a fascinating and important question for social research and social policy, but the changes in social behavior, and the variations in the changes by ethnicity, are just as interesting and just as crucial. If we are to comprehend the social meaning of America, in all of its violence, conflict, accommodation, and progress, these are the questions we must ask.

NOTES

1. Jesse Chickering (1848, p. 56) provided an early look at the phenomenon of immigration and its effect on American society. See also the discussion in Gordon (1964, pp. 94–95).

2. See Horace Kallen (1924, 1956). I am indebted to Milton Gordon for his concise sociological appraisal of Kallen's ideas. See Gordon (1964, pp. 141–149).

3. Here I differ with Pierre van den Berghe (1967, 1970) and others and follow the argument first posed by Milton Gordon (1964). Gordon's (pp. 19–59) conceptualization of ethnicity is presented only in the American context, but it embraces the categories of race, religion, and national origin. Van den Berghe, on the other hand, defines ethnicity only in terms of religion or national origin (1967, pp. 9–10), and treats race separately. His argument is based on the distinctions made between social definitions arising from *cultural* criteria (e.g., *ethnic* groups from different religions, languages, and nationality backgrounds) and social definitions founded on *physical* criteria (e.g., *racial* groups from different genetic backgrounds). There are a number of problems arising from this conceptualization, some of which van den Berghe himself notes, but the greater difficulty is the common inability to distinguish between physical and cultural definitions and group identities, and the fact that they often overlap. Two different cultural groups that share the same physical background (e.g., Catholics and Protestants in Northern Ireland) may be defined as visible to each other on the basis of quasi-physical characteristics (gestures, walk, speech) if the competition between them is intense enough. Under certain conditions, cultural differences may generate, or be expected to generate, anticipated physical differences to further the disparity between conflicting groups within the same society. Similarly, two different physical groups that share the same cultural background (Afro-American blacks and Anglo-American whites in the South of the United States) are not only visible to each other on the basis of race but also generate subcultural differences developing out of their segregation. In any event, it is difficult to speak about societal definitions of physical and cultural differences as though they were mutually exclusive. Ethnicity, in Gordon's sense and definition, is a quality of distinct peoplehood which can develop out of physical and/or cultural characteristics, depending on the situation in time and place.

4. See the brief exploration in Chapter One for some review of this question. See also Horowitz (1966) for an intriguing essay on the roles of ideology in Canada and the United States. Horowitz argues that ideological diversity in the United States is not accepted as legitimate, as it is in Canada, and this helps to explain the different states of organized socialism in the two countries. Might it not also be argued that the idea of ethnic diversity has more legitimacy in Canada as well? See Porter (1965) on the interaction of ethnicity and class in Canadian society.

5. Gordon defines "ethclass" as the "subsociety created by the intersection of the vertical stratifications of ethnicity with the horizontal stratifications

of social class. . . . Thus a person's *ethclass* might be upper-middle class white Protestant, or lower-middle class white Irish Catholic, or upper-lower class Negro Protestant, and so on." See Gordon (1964, p. 51).

6. Ethnicity may be found to be more salient at the lower class levels because the poor have little else with which to identify and also because social mobility in America has often required an exchange of values and behavior for getting ahead. On this latter point, see Novak (1971). Ethnicity may also be less visible among the middle classes but it is presumably still a force, although we don't know how much of a force. In the suburbs, for example, ethnicity persists (Gans, 1967, p. 162), and differentiation between suburban communities is more reality than myth (Berger, 1968).

7. John Higham's (1963) work constitutes the first major analysis of American society in terms of ethnic cleavage rather than in terms of class or sectional division (see also Kolodny, 1969). Ethnic violence per se (between groups of differing racial, religious, and national origins) is beginning to be documented (see Hofstadter and Wallace, 1970). A student of sociology and history, Deena Steinberg (1970), found 290 reported instances of collective violence in selected secondary sources (published monographs) between the years 1800 and 1967. These reports were classified according to the themes and clues presented in the secondary accounts: economic, political, religious, racial, national origin, or combinations of these. Of the 290 cases, 203, or 70 per cent, involved ethnic differences (religious, racial, national origin, or combinations including these ethnic factors).

APPENDIX

Table 41.   Regional Composition of Sees and Dioceses, Selected for
Calculation of Parish and Cleric Ratios[a]

Country or Province	Sees and Dioceses
Germany	Bamberg: Eichstatt, Speyer, Würzburg
	Cologne: Aachen, Limburg, Münster, Osnabrück, Trier, Essen[b]
	Freiburg: Mainz, Rottenburg
	Munich and Freising: Augsburg, Passau, Regensburg
Ireland	Cashel and Emly: Cloyne, Cork, Kerry, Killaloe, Limerick, Ross, Waterford and Lismore
	Dublin: Ferns, Ossory, Kildare and Leighlin
	Tuam: Achonry, Clonfert, Elphin, Killala, Galway and Kilmacduah with Kilfenore
Mexico (1949, 1953, 1957)	Angelopoli: Huejutla, Huajuapam de León Antequera
	Oaxaca: Chiapas, Tapachula
	Durango: Chihuahua, Sinaloa, Sonora
	Guadalajara: Aguascalientes, Colima, Tepic, Zacatecas
	Mexico: Chilapa, Cuernavaca, Tulancingo, Toluca[c]
	Monterrey:[c] Saltillo, San Luis Potosí, Tamaulipas
	Morelia: León, Querétaro, Tacambaro, Zamora
	Veracruz: Tehuantepec, Papantla[c]
	Yucatán: Campeche, Tabasco
Mexico (1961)	Antequera, Oaxaca: Chiapas, Tapachula, Tehuantepec
	Chihuahua: Ciudad Juárez, Ciudad Obregón, Hermosillo
	Durango: Culiacán, Mazatlán, Torreón
	Guadalajara: Aguascalientes, Colima, Tepic, Zacatecas
	Mexico: Acapulco, Chilapa, Cuernavaca, Texcoco, Toluca, Tulancingo
	Monterrey: Matamoros, Saltillo, San Luis Potosí, Tampico
	Morelia: León, Querétaro, Tacambaro, Zamora
	Puebla de Los Angeles: Huejutla, Huajuapam de León
	Veracruz: Papantla, San Andrés Tuxtla
	Yucatán: Campeche, Tabasco
Poland	Kraków: Częstochowa, Katowice (Stalinogród), Kielce, Tarnow
	Gniezno: Poznań, Chelmno, Wloclawek
	Lvov (U.S.S.R.): Przemysl
	Warsaw: Lódź, Lublin, Plock, Sandomierz, Siedlce
	Vilna (Vilnius, U.S.S.R.): Lomza
Puerto Rico	San Juan de Puerto Rico: Ponce, Arecibo[b]
Québec	Montréal: Joliette, Saint-Jean, Saint-Jérôme de Terrebonne,[c] Valleyfield
	Québec: Amos, Chicoutimi, Sainte-Anne-de-la-Pocatière,[c] Trois-Rivières
	Rimouski: Gaspé, Gulf of St. Lawrence

Table 41.   (Continued)

Country or Province	Sees and Dioceses
Sicily	Sherbrooke: Nicolet, Saint Hyacinthe Catania: Acireale Messina: Lipari, Nicosia, Patti Monreale: Agrigento, Caltanisseta Palermo: Cefalù, Mazara del Vallo, Trapani Siracusa: Caltagirone, Noto, Piazza Armerina, Ragusa[c]

[a] Source: *Annuario Pontificio*, 1949, 1953, 1957, 1961. All sees and dioceses are listed for all four editions and years selected, unless otherwise indicated.
[b] Listed only in 1961.
[c] Listed only in 1953, 1957, and 1961.

Table 42.   Total Raw Figure Estimates of Catholic Population, Number of Parishes, and Clerics, for Selected Geographical Regions and Years[a]

Country or Province	Year	Catholic Population	Number of Parishes	Number of Clerics
Germany	1949	19,508,796	8,978	22,626
	1953	20,268,063	9,300	24,006
	1957	21,209,835	9,614	24,333
	1961	22,301,885	9,935	25,383
Ireland	1949	2,259,222	743	5,338
	1953	2,302,224	748	5,615
	1957	2,309,454	753	6,026
	1961	2,116,817	699	5,943
Mexico	1949	19,858,974	1,929	5,672
	1953	23,604,468	2,087	7,075
	1957	25,159,048	2,138	8,114
	1961	30,051,667	2,071	8,217
Poland	1949	19,523,719	5,357	11,718
	1953	19,053,057	5,674	12,753
	1957	18,731,356	5,121	14,286
	1961	17,772,407	5,036	13,601
Puerto Rico	1949	1,830,000	99	281
	1953	2,125,000	106	328
	1957	2,050,000	111	393
	1961	2,400,000	117	485
Quebec	1949	2,933,772	1,353	7,032
	1953	3,250,963	1,461	7,643
	1957	3,605,636	1,550	8,261
	1961	3,963,114	1,637	9,065

Table 42.   (Continued)

Sicily	1949	4,188,975	1,119	5,133
	1953	4,429,372	1,179	5,219
	1957	4,582,663	1,259	4,748
	1961	4,695,353	1,342	4,927

[a] Source: *Annuario Pontificio*, 1949, 1953, 1957, 1961. The estimated figures are the reported totals of designated sees and dioceses, as shown in Appendix Table 41.

REFERENCES

Abramson, Harold J. "Ethnic Diversity within Catholicism: A Comparative Analysis of Contemporary and Historical Religion," *Journal of Social History*, 4 (Summer 1971), 359–388.

Abramson, Harold J. *The Ethnic Factor in American Catholicism: An Analysis of Inter-ethnic Marriage and Religious Involvement*. Unpublished Ph.D. dissertation, University of Chicago, 1969.

Abramson, Harold J. "Inter-ethnic Marriage among Catholic Americans and Changes in Religious Behavior," *Sociological Analysis*, 32 (Spring 1971), 31–44.

Abramson, Harold J. and C. Edward Noll. "Religion, Ethnicity and Social Change," *Review of Religious Research*, 8 (Fall 1966), 11–26.

Allswang, John M. *A House for All Peoples: Ethnic Politics in Chicago 1890–1936*. Lexington: The University Press of Kentucky, 1971.

Anderson, Charles H. *White Protestant Americans: From National Origins to Religious Group*. Englewood Cliffs, N.J.: Prentice-Hall, 1970.

Anderson, Elin. *We Americans*. Cambridge: Harvard University Press, 1938.

Annuario Pontificio. 1949, 1953, 1957, 1961. Citta del Vaticano.

Argyle, W. J. "European Nationalism and African Tribalism," in P. H. Gulliver (ed.), *Tradition and Transition in East Africa: Studies of the Tribal Element in the Modern Era*. London: Routledge and Kegan Paul, 1969, 41–57.

Balch, Emily Greene. *Our Slavic Fellow Citizens*. New York: Charities Publication Committee, 1910.

Baltzell, E. Digby. *The Protestant Establishment: Aristocracy and Caste in America*. New York: Random House Vintage Books, 1966.

Banfield, Edward C. *The Moral Basis of a Backward Society*. New York: Free Press, 1958.

Baron, Salo W. *Modern Nationalism and Religion*. New York: Meridian Books, 1960.

Barry, Colman J. *The Catholic Church and German Americans*. Washington: Catholic University of America Press, 1953.

Bass, Herbert J. (ed.). *The State of American History*. Chicago: Quadrangle, 1970.

Bender, Eugene I. and George Kagiwada. "Hansen's Law of 'Third-Generation Return' and the Study of American Religio-Ethnic Groups," *Phylon*, 29 (Winter 1968), 360–370.

Berger, Bennett M. "Suburbia and the American Dream," in Sylvia Fleis Fava (ed.), *Urbanism in World Perspective*. New York: Thomas Y. Crowell, 1968, 434–444.

Berger, Morroe, Theodore Abel, and Charles H. Page (eds.). *Freedom and Control in Modern Society*. New York: Van Nostrand, 1954.

Berkowitz, Morris I. and J. Edmund Johnson. *Social Scientific Studies of Religion: A Bibliography*. Pittsburgh: University of Pittsburgh Press, 1967.

Billington, Ray Allen. *The Protestant Crusade: 1800–1860*. Chicago: Quadrangle, 1964.

Birmingham, Stephen. *"Our Crowd": The Great Jewish Families of New York*. New York: Harper and Row, 1966.

Blalock, Hubert M., Jr. *Toward a Theory of Minority-Group Relations*. New York: John Wiley and Sons, 1967.

Blanshard, Paul. *American Freedom and Catholic Power*. Boston: Beacon Press, 1949.

Blauner, Robert. "Internal Colonialism and Ghetto Revolt," *Social Problems*, 16 (Spring 1969), 393–408.

Bourne, Randolph. *History of a Literary Radical and Other Essays*, edited by Van Wyck Brooks. New York: B. W. Huebsch, 1920.

Brown, Thomas N. *Irish-American Nationalism 1870–1890*. Philadelphia: J. B. Lippincott, 1966.

Browne, Henry J. "The 'Italian Problem' in the Catholic Church of the United States, 1880–1900," *United States Catholic Historical Society, Historical Records and Studies*, 35 (1946), 46–72.

Bryce, James. *The American Commonwealth*, Vol. II. New York: Macmillan, 1917.

Buchanan, John T. "How to Assimilate the Foreign Element in Our Population," *Forum*, 32 (February 1902), 686–694.

Burns, R. E. "Parsons, Priests, and the People: The Rise of Irish Anti-Clericalism 1785–1789," *Church History*, 31 (March 1962), 151–163.

Cahnman, Werner J. "Religion and Nationality," in Werner J. Cahnman and Alvin Boskoff (eds.), *Sociology and History*. New York: Free Press, 1964, 271–280.

Cahnman, Werner J. and Alvin Boskoff (eds.). *Sociology and History*. New York: Free Press, 1964.

Chickering, Jesse. *Immigration into the United States*. Boston: Charles C. Little and James Brown, 1848.

Christian, Jane Macnab and Chester C. Christian, Jr. "Spanish Language and Culture in the Southwest," in Joshua A. Fishman, et al., *Language Loyalty in the United States*. The Hague: Mouton, 1966, 280–317.

Clancy, William P. "Catholicism in America," in *The Commonweal* (ed.), *Catholicism in America*. New York: Harcourt, Brace, 1953, 9–24.

Clark, Kenneth B. *Dark Ghetto*. New York: Harper Torchbooks, 1967.

Clark, William Lloyd. *The Story of My Battle with the Scarlet Beast*. Milan, Ill.: The Rail Splitter Press, 1932.

Cohen, Abner. *Custom and Politics in Urban Africa: A Study of Hausa Migrants in Yoruba Towns*. Berkeley: University of California Press, 1969.

Cole, William I. "Two Ancient Faiths," in Robert A. Woods (ed.), *Americans in Process*. Boston: Houghton Mifflin, 1903, 254–288.

Coles, Robert and Jon Erikson. *The Middle Americans*. Boston: Little, Brown, 1971.

The Commonweal (ed.). *Catholicism in America*. New York: Harcourt, Brace, 1953.

Cornelisen, Ann. *Torregreca: Life, Death, Miracles*. Boston: Little, Brown, 1969.

Covello, Leonard. *The Social Background of the Italo-American School Child*. Leiden: E. J. Brill, 1967.

Cross, Robert D. *The Emergence of Liberal Catholicism in America*. Cambridge: Harvard University Press, 1958.

Davis, Kingsley. "Intermarriage in Caste Societies," *American Anthropologist*, 43 (1941), 376–395.

Demerath, N. J., III. *Social Class in American Protestantism*. Chicago: Rand McNally, 1965.

Deutsch, Karl W. *Nationalism and Social Communication*. Cambridge: The M.I.T. Press, 2nd ed., 1966.

Dotson, Floyd and Lillian O. Dotson. *The Indian Minority of Zambia, Rhodesia, and Malawi*. New Haven: Yale University Press, 1968.

Drachsler, Julius. *Intermarriage in New York City*. New York: Columbia University, 1921.

Ducharme, Jacques. *The Delusson Family*. New York: Funk and Wagnalls, 1939.

Ducharme, Jacques. *The Shadows of the Trees*. New York: Harper and Brothers, 1943.

Dumont, Fernand. "The Systematic Study of the French-Canadian Total Society," in Marcel Rioux and Yves Martin (eds.), *French-Canadian Society*, Vol. I. Toronto: McClelland and Stewart, 1965, 386–405.

Duncan, O. D. "A Socio-economic Index for All Occupations," in Albert J. Reiss, Jr. (ed.), *Occupations and Social Status*. New York: Free Press of Glencoe, 1961, 109–161.

Easton, David and Jack Dennis. *Children in the Political System*. New York: McGraw-Hill, 1969.

Eisenstadt, S. N. *The Absorption of Immigrants*. London: Routledge and Kegan Paul, 1954.

Ellis, John Tracy. "American Catholics and the Intellectual Life," *Thought*, 30 (Autumn 1955), 351–388.

Farlardeau, Jean-Charles. "The Role and Importance of the Church in French Canada," in Marcel Rioux and Yves Martin (eds.), *French-Canadian Society*, Vol. I. Toronto: McClelland and Stewart, 1965, 342–357.

Fava, Sylvia Fleis (ed.). *Urbanism in World Perspective*. New York: Thomas Y. Crowell, 1968.

Feinstein, Otto (ed.). *Ethnic Groups in the City*. Lexington, Mass.: Heath Lexington Books, 1971.

Fichter, Joseph H. "The Americanization of Catholicism," in Thomas T. McAvoy (ed.), *Roman Catholicism and the American Way of Life*. Notre Dame, Ind.: University of Notre Dame Press, 1960, 113–127.

Fichter, Joseph H. *Parochial School: A Sociological Study*. Garden City, N. Y.: Doubleday, 1964.

Fichter, Joseph H. "The Profile of Catholic Religious Life," *American Journal of Sociology*, 58 (1952), 145–149.

Fichter, Joseph H. *Social Relations in the Urban Parish*. Chicago: University of Chicago Press, 1954.

Finestone, Harold. *A Comparative Study of Reformation and Recidivism among Italian and Polish Criminal Offenders*. Unpublished Ph.D. dissertation, University of Chicago, 1963.

Fishman, Joshua A. et al. *Language Loyalty in the United States*. The Hague: Mouton, 1966.

Fishman, Joshua A. and John E. Hofman. "Mother Tongue and Nativity in the American Population," in Joshua A. Fishman et al., *Language Loyalty in the United States*. The Hague: Mouton, 1966, 34–50.

Fitzpatrick, Joseph P. "Intermarriage of Puerto Ricans in New York City," *American Journal of Sociology*, 71 (January 1966), 395–406.

Fitzpatrick, Joseph P. "Mexicans and Puerto Ricans Build a Bridge," *America*, 94 (December 31, 1955), 373–375.

Fitzpatrick, Joseph P. *Puerto Rican Americans: The Meaning of Migration to the Mainland*. Englewood Cliffs, N. J.: Prentice-Hall, 1971.

Foerster, Robert F. *The Italian Emigration of Our Times*. Cambridge: Harvard University Press, 1919.

Fogarty, Michael P. *Christian Democracy in Western Europe 1820–1953*. London: Routledge and Kegan Paul, 1957.

Francis, E. K. "The Nature of the Ethnic Group," *American Journal of Sociology*, 52 (March 1947), 393–400.

Fuchs, Lawrence H. *Political Behavior of American Jews*. Glencoe, Ill.: The Free Press, 1956.

Gans, Herbert J. *The Levittowners: Ways of Life and Politics in a New Suburban Community*. New York: Pantheon Books, 1967.

Gans, Herbert J. *The Urban Villagers: Group and Class in the Life of Italian-Americans*. New York: Free Press of Glencoe, 1962.

Gittler, Joseph B. (ed.). *Understanding Minority Groups*. New York: John Wiley and Sons, 1956.

Glazer, Nathan. *American Judaism*. Chicago: University of Chicago Press, 1957.

Glazer, Nathan. "Ethnic Groups in America," in Morroe Berger, Theodore Abel, and Charles H. Page (eds.), *Freedom and Control in Modern Society*. New York: Van Nostrand, 1954, 158–173.

Glazer, Nathan and Daniel Patrick Moynihan. *Beyond the Melting Pot*. Cambridge: The M.I.T. Press, 1963 (1st ed.), 1970 (2nd ed.).

Gleason, Philip. *The Conservative Reformers: German-American Catholics and the Social Order*. Notre Dame, Ind.: University of Notre Dame Press, 1968.

Glock, Charles Y. and Rodney Stark. *Religion and Society in Tension*. Chicago: Rand McNally, 1965.

Goldman, Eric F. *Rendezvous with Destiny*. New York: Alfred A. Knopf, 1952.

Gordon, Milton M. *Assimilation in American Life*. New York: Oxford University Press, 1964.

Gossett, Thomas F. *Race: The History of an Idea in America*. New York: Schocken Books, 1965.

Grebler, Leo et al. *The Mexican-American People: The Nation's Second Largest Minority*. New York: The Free Press, 1970.

Greeley, Andrew M. *The Catholic Experience*. Garden City, N. Y.: Doubleday Image Books, 1969.

Greeley, Andrew M. *Religion and Career*. New York: Sheed and Ward, 1963.

Greeley, Andrew M. *Why Can't They Be like Us?* New York: E. P. Dutton, 1971.

Greeley, Andrew M. and Peter H. Rossi. *The Education of Catholic Americans*. Chicago: Aldine, 1966.

Greene, Victor R. *The Slavic Community on Strike: Immigrant Labor in Pennsylvania Anthracite*. Notre Dame, Ind.: University of Notre Dame Press, 1968.

Gulliver, P. H. (ed.). *Tradition and Transition in East Africa: Studies of the Tribal Element in the Modern Era*. London: Routledge and Kegan Paul, 1969.

Hadden, Jeffrey K. *The Gathering Storm in the Churches*. Garden City, N. Y.: Doubleday, 1969.

Haerle, Rudolf K., Jr. *A Survey of the Literature on Religious Intermarriage, with Special Emphasis on Catholics in Mixed Marriage*. Unpublished M.A. thesis, University of Chicago, 1962.

Handlin, Oscar. *The Uprooted*. New York: Grosset and Dunlap, 1951.

Handlin, Oscar (ed.). *Immigration as a Factor in American History*. Englewood Cliffs, N. J.: Prentice-Hall, 1959.

Hansen, Marcus Lee. *The Atlantic Migration 1607–1860*. Cambridge: Harvard University Press, 1940.

Hansen, Marcus Lee. *The Problem of the Third Generation Immigrant*. Rock Island, Ill.: Augustana Historical Society, 1938.

Hansen, Marcus Lee. "The Third Generation in America," *Commentary*, 14 (November 1952), 492–500.

Harris, Marvin. "Caste, Class, and Minority," *Social Forces*, 37 (March 1959), 248–254.

Haugen, Einar. *The Norwegian Language in America*, Vol. I. Philadelphia: University of Pennsylvania Press, 1953.

Hawgood, John A. *The Tragedy of German-America*. New York: G. P. Putnam's Sons, 1940.

Heiss, Jerold S. "Interfaith Marriage and Marital Outcome," *Marriage and Family Living*, 23 (August 1961), 228–233.

Heiss, Jerold S. "Premarital Characteristics of the Religiously Intermarried in an Urban Area," *American Sociological Review*, 25 (February 1960), 47–55.

Herberg, Will. *Protestant-Catholic-Jew*. Garden City, N.Y.: Doubleday, 1955.

Higham, John. *Strangers in the Land: Patterns of American Nativism 1860–1925*. New York: Atheneum, 1963.

Hofstadter, Richard. *Anti-intellectualism in American Life*. New York: Alfred A. Knopf, 1969.

Hofstadter, Richard and Michael Wallace (eds.). *American Violence: A Documentary History*. New York: Alfred A. Knopf, 1970.

Hollingshead, August B. "Cultural Factors in the Selection of Marriage Mates," *American Sociological Review*, 15 (October 1950), 619–627.

Horowitz, G. "Conservatism, Liberalism, and Socialism in Canada: An Interpretation," *Canadian Journal of Economics and Political Science*, 32 (May 1966), 143–171.

Houtart, François and Émile Pin. *The Church and the Latin American Revolution*. New York: Sheed and Ward, 1965.

Hughes, Everett C. *French Canada in Transition*. Chicago: University of Chicago Press, 1963.

Hutchinson, Edward P. *Immigrants and Their Children*. New York: John Wiley and Sons, 1956.

Industrial Relations Research Association (ed.). *Manpower in the United States: Problems and Policies*. New York: Harper and Brothers, 1954.

Iwanska, Alicja (ed.). *Contemporary Poland: Society, Politics, Economy*. Chicago: University of Chicago, Human Relations Area Files, 1955.

Janowitz, Morris. *Sociology and the Military Establishment*. New York: Russell Sage Foundation, 1959.

Jemolo, A. C. *Church and State in Italy 1850–1950*. Oxford: Basil Blackwell, 1960.

Jensen, Merrill (ed.). *Regionalism in America*. Madison: University of Wisconsin Press, 1951.

Johnstone, John C., Jean-Claude Willig, and Joseph M. Spina. *Young People's Images of Canadian Society*. Ottawa: Studies of the Royal Commission on Bilingualism and Biculturalism, 1969.

Kallen, Horace M. *Cultural Pluralism and the American Idea*. Philadelphia: University of Pennsylvania Press, 1956.

Kallen, Horace M. *Culture and Democracy in the United States*. New York: Boni and Liveright, 1924.

Kantrowitz, Nathan. "Ethnic and Racial Segregation in the New York Metropolis, 1960," *American Journal of Sociology*, 74 (May 1969), 685–695.

Kennedy, Ruby Jo Reeves. "Residential Propinquity and Ethnic Endogamy," *American Journal of Sociology*, 48 (March 1943), 580–584.

Kennedy, Ruby Jo Reeves. "Single or Triple Melting-Pot? Intermarriage Trends in New Haven, 1870-1940, "*American Journal of Sociology*, 49 (January 1944), 331–339.

Kennedy, Ruby Jo Reeves. "Single or Triple Melting-Pot? Intermarriage in New Haven, 1870–1950," *American Journal of Sociology,* 58 (July 1952), 56–59.

Killian, Lewis M. *White Southerners*. New York: Random House, 1970.

Kitano, Harry H. L. *Japanese Americans: The Evolution of a Subculture*. Englewood Cliffs, N.J.: Prentice-Hall, 1969.

Kloss, Heinz. "German-American Language Maintenance Efforts," in Joshua A. Fishman et al., *Language Loyalty in the United States*. The Hague: Mouton, 1966, 206–252.

Kohn, Hans. *Nationalism: Its Meaning and History*. New York: Van Nostrand, 1956.

Kolarz, Walter. *Myths and Realities in Eastern Europe*. London: Lindsay Drummond, 1946.

Kolodny, Ralph L. "Ethnic Cleavages in the United States," *Social Work*, 14 (January 1969), 13–23.

Kuper, Leo and M. G. Smith (eds.). *Pluralism in Africa*. Berkeley: University of California Press, 1969.

LaFarge, John. "The American Catholic," in Joseph B. Gittler (ed.), *Understanding Minority Groups*. New York: John Wiley and Sons, 1956, 17–32.

Larkin, Emmet. "Church and State in Ireland in the Nineteenth Century," *Church History*, 31 (September 1962), 294–306.

Larkin, Emmet. "Economic Growth, Capital Investment, and the Roman Catholic Church in Nineteenth-Century Ireland," *American Historical Review*, 72 (April 1967), 852–875.

Larkin, Emmet. *James Larkin: Irish Labour Leader 1876–1947*. Cambridge: The M.I.T. Press, 1965.

Larkin, Emmet. "Socialism and Catholicism in Ireland," *Church History*, 33 (December 1964), 462–483.

Latourette, Kenneth Scott. *Christianity in a Revolutionary Age*, Vol. I, II, III, IV, V. New York: Harper and Brothers, 1958–1962.

Lazerwitz, Bernard and Louis Rowitz. "The Three-Generations Hypothesis," *American Journal of Sociology,* 69 (March 1964), 529–538.

Lemaire, Herve-B. "Franco-American Efforts on Behalf of the French Language in New England," in Joshua A. Fishman et al., *Language Loyalty in the United States*. The Hague: Mouton, 1966, 253–279.

Lenski, Gerhard. *The Religious Factor*. Garden City, N.Y.: Doubleday, 1961.

Levi, Carlo. *Christ Stopped at Eboli*. New York: Farrar, Straus, 1947.

Lévi-Strauss, Claude. *The Elementary Structures of Kinship*. Boston: Beacon Press, 1969.

Levy, Mark R. and Michael S. Kramer. *The Ethnic Factor: How America's Minorities Decide Elections*. New York: Simon and Schuster, 1972.

Lieberson, Stanley. *Ethnic Patterns in American Cities*. New York: Free Press of Glencoe, 1963.

Lieberson, Stanley. *Language and Ethnic Relations in Canada.* New York: John Wiley and Sons, 1970.

Linton, Ralph (ed.). *The Science of Man in the World Crisis.* New York: Columbia University Press, 1945.

Linton, Ralph. *The Study of Man.* New York: Appleton-Century, 1936.

Liu, William T. and Nathaniel J. Pallone (eds.). *Catholics/U.S.A.* New York: John Wiley and Sons, 1970.

Lopreato, Joseph. *Italian Americans.* New York: Random House, 1970.

Luebke, Frederick C. *Immigrants and Politics: The Germans of Nebraska, 1880-1900.* Lincoln: University of Nebraska Press, 1969.

Mack Smith, Denis. *Italy: A Modern History.* Ann Arbor: University of Michigan Press, 1959.

Martineau, Harriet. *Society in America*, Vol. II. Paris: Baudry's European Library, 1837.

McAvoy, Thomas T. (ed.). *Roman Catholicism and the American Way of Life.* Notre Dame, Ind.: University of Notre Dame Press, 1960.

McHale, Tom. *Principato.* New York: Viking, 1970.

Mecham, J. Lloyd. *Church and State in Latin America.* Chapel Hill: University of North Carolina Press, 1934.

Melville, Herman. *Redburn: His First Voyage.* Boston: L. C. Page, 1924; originally published in 1849.

Merton, Robert K. "Intermarriage and the Social Structure: Fact and Theory," *Psychiatry*, 4 (August 1941), 361-374.

Mills, C. Wright, Clarence Senior, and Rose Kohn Goldsen. *The Puerto Rican Journey.* New York: Harper, 1950.

Miner, Horace M. *St. Denis, a French-Canadian Parish.* Chicago: University of Chicago Press, 1939.

Mittelbach, Frank G. and Joan W. Moore. "Ethnic Endogamy—The Case of Mexican Americans," *American Journal of Sociology*, 74 (July 1968), 50-62.

Morse, Jedidiah. *The American Geography.* Elizabethtown, N.J.: privately printed, 1789.

Murdock, George P. *Social Structure.* New York: Macmillan, 1960.

Nahirny, Vladimir C. and Joshua A. Fishman. "Ukrainian Language Maintenance Efforts in the United States," in Joshua A. Fishman et al., *Language Loyalty in the United States.* The Hague: Mouton, 1966, 318-357.

Nelson, Lowry. "Speaking of Tongues," *American Journal of Sociology*, 54 (November 1948), 202-210.

Niebuhr, H. Richard. *The Social Sources of Denominationalism.* New York: Henry Holt, 1929; and Cleveland: World Publishing, Meridian Books, 1957.

Novak, Michael. *The Rise of the Unmeltable Ethnics: Politics and Culture in the Seventies.* New York: Macmillan, 1971.

Nuesse, C. J. and Thomas J. Harte (eds.). *The Sociology of the Parish.* Milwaukee: Bruce, 1951.

O'Dea, Thomas F. *American Catholic Dilemma.* New York: Sheed and Ward, 1958.

O'Dea, Thomas F. "The Catholic Immigrant and the American Scene," *Thought*, 31 (Summer 1956), 251-270.

Odum, Howard W. and Harry E. Moore. *American Regionalism.* New York: Henry Holt, 1938.

O'Faolain, Sean. *The Irish: A Character Study*. New York: Devin-Adair, 1949.

Official Catholic Directory, 1964, 1970. New York: P. J. Kenedy and Sons, 1964, 1970.

Padilla, Elena. *Up from Puerto Rico*. New York: Columbia University Press, 1958.

Palmer, Gladys L. and Ann R. Miller. "The Occupational and Industrial Distribution of Employment, 1910–50," in Industrial Relations Research Association (ed.), *Manpower in the United States: Problems and Policies*. New York: Harper and Brothers, 1954.

Panunzio, Constantine M. *The Soul of an Immigrant*. New York: Macmillan, 1921.

Parenti, Michael. "Ethnic Politics and the Persistence of Ethnic Identification," *American Political Science Review*, 61 (September 1967), 717–726.

Park, Robert E. and Herbert A. Miller. *Old World Traits Transplanted*. New York: Harper and Brothers, 1921.

Parsons, Talcott, et al. (eds.). *Theories of Society: Foundations of Modern Sociological Theory*, Vol. I. New York: Free Press of Glencoe, 1961.

Pike, Frederick B. (ed.). *The Conflict between Church and State in Latin America*. New York: Alfred A. Knopf, 1964.

Pin, Émile. *Pratique Religieuse et Classes Sociales dans une Paroisse Urbaine Saint-Pothin à Lyon*. Paris: Éditions Spes, 1956.

Porter, John. *The Vertical Mosaic: An Analysis of Social Class and Power in Canada*. Toronto: University of Toronto Press, 1965.

Potter, George W. *To the Golden Door*. Boston: Little, Brown, 1960.

Rama, Carlos M. "Pasado y Presente de la Religion en America Latina," *Cuadernos Americanos*, 26 (July-August 1967), 25–43.

Reiss, Albert J., Jr. (ed.). *Occupations and Social Status*. New York: Free Press of Glencoe, 1961.

Rioux, Marcel and Yves Martin (eds.). *French-Canadian Society*, Vol. I. Toronto: McClelland and Stewart, 1965.

Rischin, Moses. *The Promised City: New York's Jews 1870–1914*. Cambridge: Harvard University Press, 1962.

Rosen, Bernard C. Book review of Gerhard Lenski, *The Religious Factor*, in *American Sociological Review*, 27 (February 1962), 111–113.

Rosen, Bernard C. "Race, Ethnicity, and the Achievement Syndrome," *American Sociological Review*, 24 (February 1959), 47–60.

Ross, Edward A. *The Old World in the New*. New York: Century, 1914.

Ross, Edward A. *The Russian Bolshevik Revolution*. New York: Century, 1921.

Ross, Edward A. *The Russian Soviet Republic*. New York: Century, 1923.

Ross, Edward A. *Seventy Years of It*. New York: D. Appleton-Century, 1936.

Ross, Edward A. *South of Panama*. New York: Century, 1915.

Rossi, Peter H. and Alice S. Rossi. "Some Effects of Parochial School Education in America," *Daedalus*, 90 (Spring 1961), 300–328.

Rubel, Arthur J. *Across the Tracks: Mexican-Americans in a Texas City*. Austin: University of Texas Press, 1966.

Russo, Nicholas J. *The Religious Acculturation of the Italians in New York City*. Unpublished Ph.D. dissertation, St. John's University, 1968.

Russo, Nicholas J. "Three Generations of Italians in New York City: Their Religious Acculturation," in Silvano M. Tomasi and Madeline H. Engel (eds.), *The Italian Experience in the United States*. Staten Island, N.Y.: Center for Migration Studies, 1970, 195–209.

Santayana, George. *Character and Opinion in the United States*. New York: Charles Scribner's Sons, 1924.

Scagnelli, Peter J. "Ethnicity and Religion: The Case of the Polish National Catholic Church." Unpublished paper, Department of Sociology, University of Connecticut, 1970.

Schermerhorn, R. A. *Comparative Ethnic Relations*. New York: Random House, 1970.

Schnepp, Gerald J. and Louis A. Roberts. "Residential Propinquity and Mate Selection on a Parish Basis," *American Journal of Sociology*, 58 (July 1952), 45–50.

Schrag, Peter. *The Decline of the WASP*. New York: Simon and Schuster, 1970.

Scott, John Finley. "The American College Sorority: Its Role in Class and Ethnic Endogamy," *American Sociological Review*, 30 (August 1965), 514–527.

Shannon, William V. *The American Irish*. New York: Macmillan, 1963.

Shaughnessy, Gerald. *Has the Immigrant Kept the Faith?* New York: Macmillan, 1925.

Shibutani, Tamotsu and Kian M. Kwan. *Ethnic Stratification*. New York: Macmillan, 1965.

Siegfried, André. *America Comes of Age*. New York: Harcourt, Brace, 1927.

Silone, Ignazio. *Bread and Wine*. New York: Harper and Brothers, 1937.

Smith, M. G. "Institutional and Political Conditions of Pluralism," in Leo Kuper and M. G. Smith (eds.), *Pluralism in Africa*. Berkeley: University of California Press, 1969, 27–65.

Solomon, Barbara Miller. *Ancestors and Immigrants*. Cambridge: Harvard University Press, 1956.

Steinberg, Deena J. "Historical Survey of Violence in the United States, 1800–1967." Unpublished paper, Department of Sociology, University of Connecticut, 1970.

Steward, Julian H., et al. *The People of Puerto Rico*. Champaign: University of Illinois Press, 1956.

Suttles, Gerald D. *The Social Order of the Slum*. Chicago: University of Chicago Press, 1968.

Theriault, George F. "The Franco-Americans of New England," in Mason Wade (ed.), *Canadian Dualism*. Toronto: University of Toronto Press, 1960, 392–411.

Thomas, John L. *The American Catholic Family*. Englewood Cliffs, N.J.: Prentice-Hall, 1956.

Thomas, John L. "The Factor of Religion in the Selection of Marriage Mates," *American Sociological Review,* 16 (August 1951), 487–491.

Thomas, John L. "Out-Group Marriage Patterns of Some Selected Ethnic Groups," *American Catholic Sociological Review,* 15 (March 1954), 9–18.

Thomas, W. I. and Florian Znaniecki. *The Polish Peasant in Europe and America*, Vol. II. New York: Alfred A. Knopf, 1927.

Tomasi, Silvano M. and Madeline H. Engel (eds.). *The Italian Experience in the United States*. Staten Island, N.Y.: Center for Migration Studies, 1970.

Tuck, Ruth D. *Not with the Fist*. New York: Harcourt, Brace, 1946.

U. S. Bureau of the Census. *U. S. Census of Population: 1960*, Vol. 1. Washington, D.C.: U. S. Government Printing Office, 1961.

U. S. Bureau of the Census. *Current Population Reports,* Series P-25, 1964. Washington, D.C.: U.S. Government Printing Office, 1964.

van den Berghe, Pierre L. *Race and Ethnicity*. New York: Basic Books, 1970.

van den Berghe, Pierre L. *Race and Racism*. New York: John Wiley and Sons, 1967.

Vecoli, Rudolph J. "Ethnicity: A Neglected Dimension of American History," in Herbert J. Bass (ed.), *The State of American History*. Chicago: Quadrangle, 1970, 70–88.

Vecoli, Rudolph J. "Prelates and Peasants: Italian Immigrants and the Catholic Church," *Journal of Social History*, 2 (Spring 1969), 217–268.

Verga, Giovanni. *Little Novels of Sicily*. New York: Grove Press, 1953; originally published in 1883.

Wade, Mason (ed.). *Canadian Dualism*. Toronto: University of Toronto Press, 1960.

Wade, Mason. *The French-Canadian Outlook*. New York: Viking, 1946.

Ware, Caroline F. *Greenwich Village 1920–1930*. Boston: Houghton Mifflin, 1935.

Warkov, Seymour and Andrew M. Greeley. "Parochial School Origins and Educational Achievement," *American Sociological Review*, 31 (June 1966), 406–414.

Warner, W. Lloyd and Leo Srole. *The Social Systems of American Ethnic Groups*. New Haven: Yale University Press, 1945.

Weber, Max. *Economy and Society*, Vol. 1, edited by Guenther Roth and Claus Wittich. New York: Bedminster Press, 1968.

Wessel, Bessie B. *An Ethnic Survey of Woonsocket, Rhode Island*. Chicago: University of Chicago Press, 1931.

White, Leslie A. *The Evolution of Culture*. New York: McGraw-Hill, 1959.

Wickham, E. R. *Church and People in an Industrial City*. London: Lutterworth Press, 1957.

Williams, Robin M., Jr. "Unity and Diversity in Modern America," *Social Forces*, 36 (October 1957), 1–8.

Wirth, Louis. "The Problem of Minority Groups," in Ralph Linton (ed.), *The Science of Man in the World Crisis*. New York: Columbia University Press, 1945, 347–372.

Wolfinger, Raymond E. "The Development and Persistence of Ethnic Voting," *American Political Science Review*, 59 (December 1965), 896–908.

Woodham-Smith, Cecil. *The Great Hunger: Ireland 1845–1849*. New York: Harper and Row, 1962.

Woods, Robert A. (ed.). *Americans in Process*. Boston: Houghton Mifflin, 1903.

Yinger, J. Milton. *Sociology Looks at Religion*. New York: Macmillan, 1963.

INDEX

About the Author

HAROLD J. ABRAMSON is Associate Professor of Sociology at the University of Connecticut. He received his B.A. in history and French from the University of Rochester, and his M.A. and Ph.D. degrees in sociogy from the University of Chicago where he was associated with the National Opinion Research Center and the Population Research and Training Center.